MY NAME IS

_____

I'M ___ YEARS OLD

PHONE NUMBER

_____

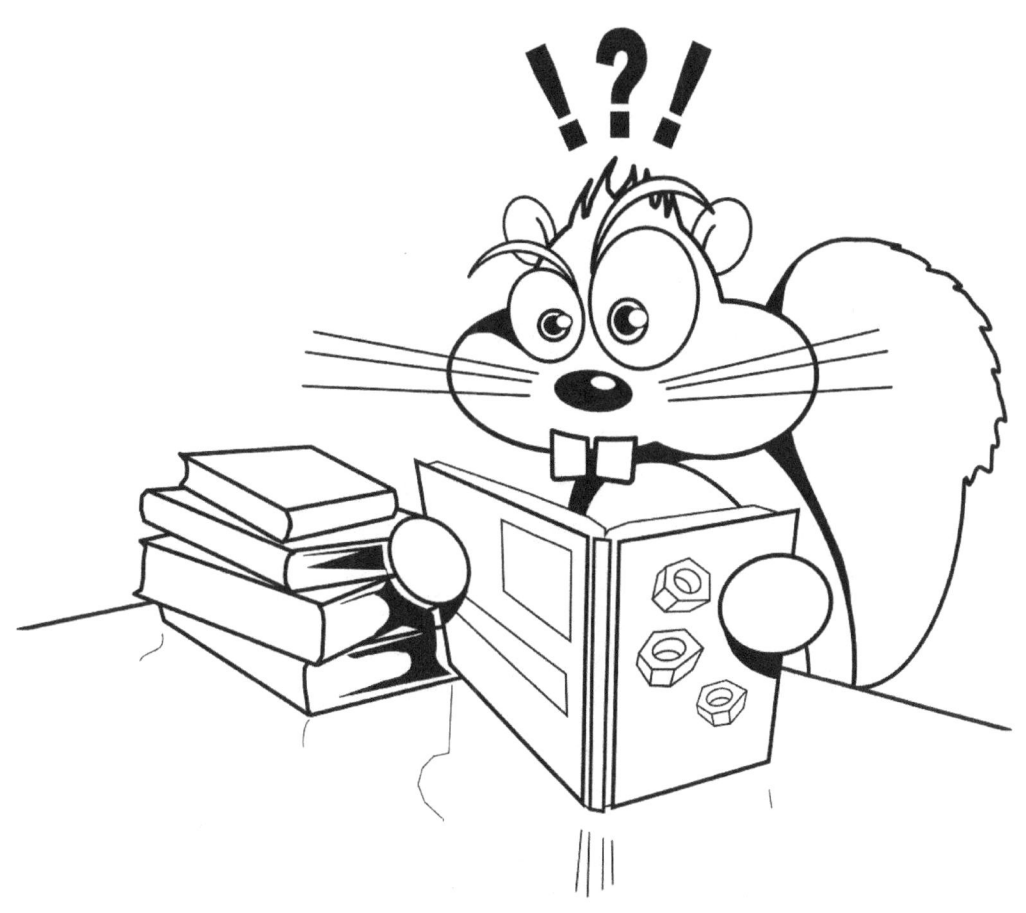

HANDWRITING , COLORING WORK BOOK

ALPHABET

SAY & COLOR

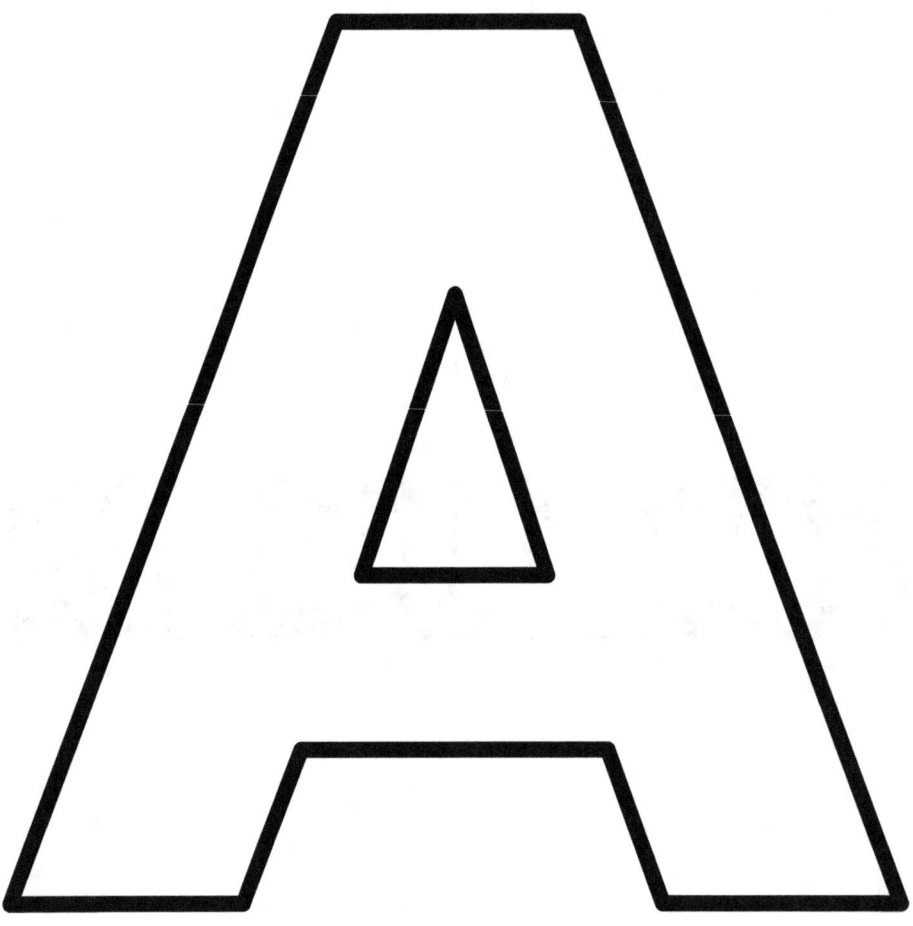

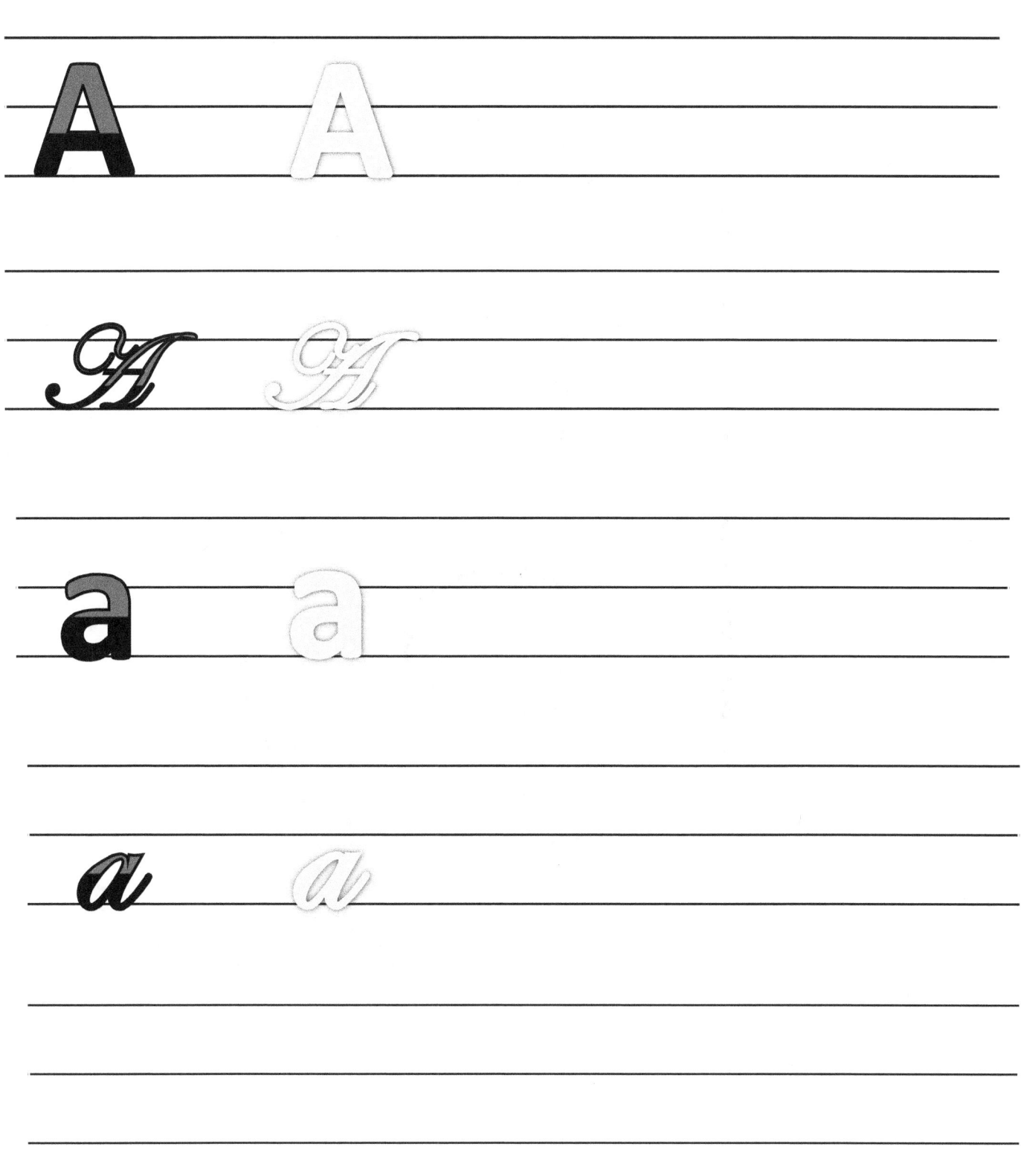

SAY & COLOR

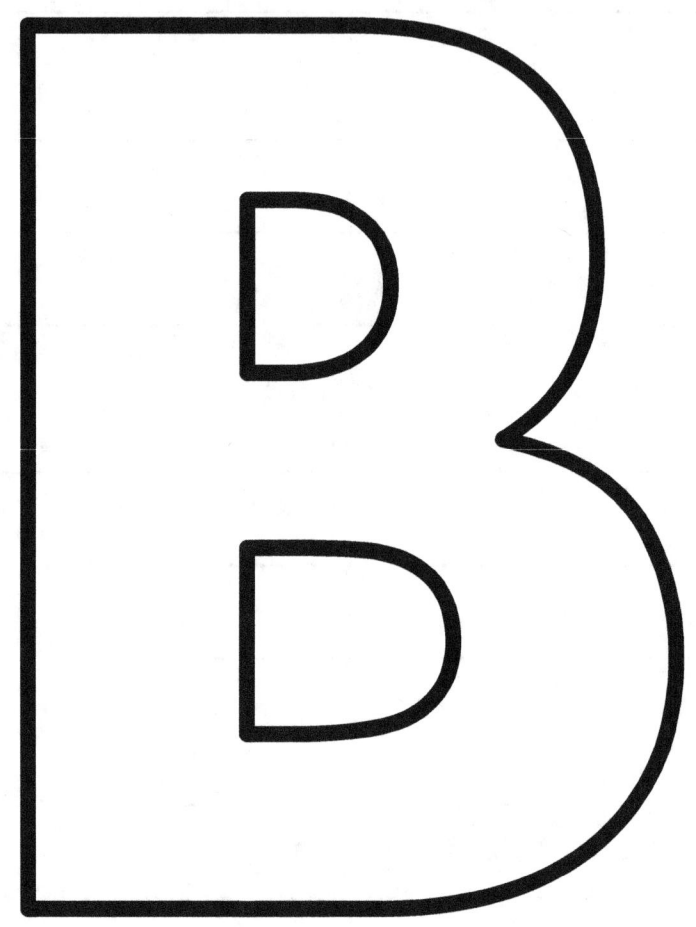

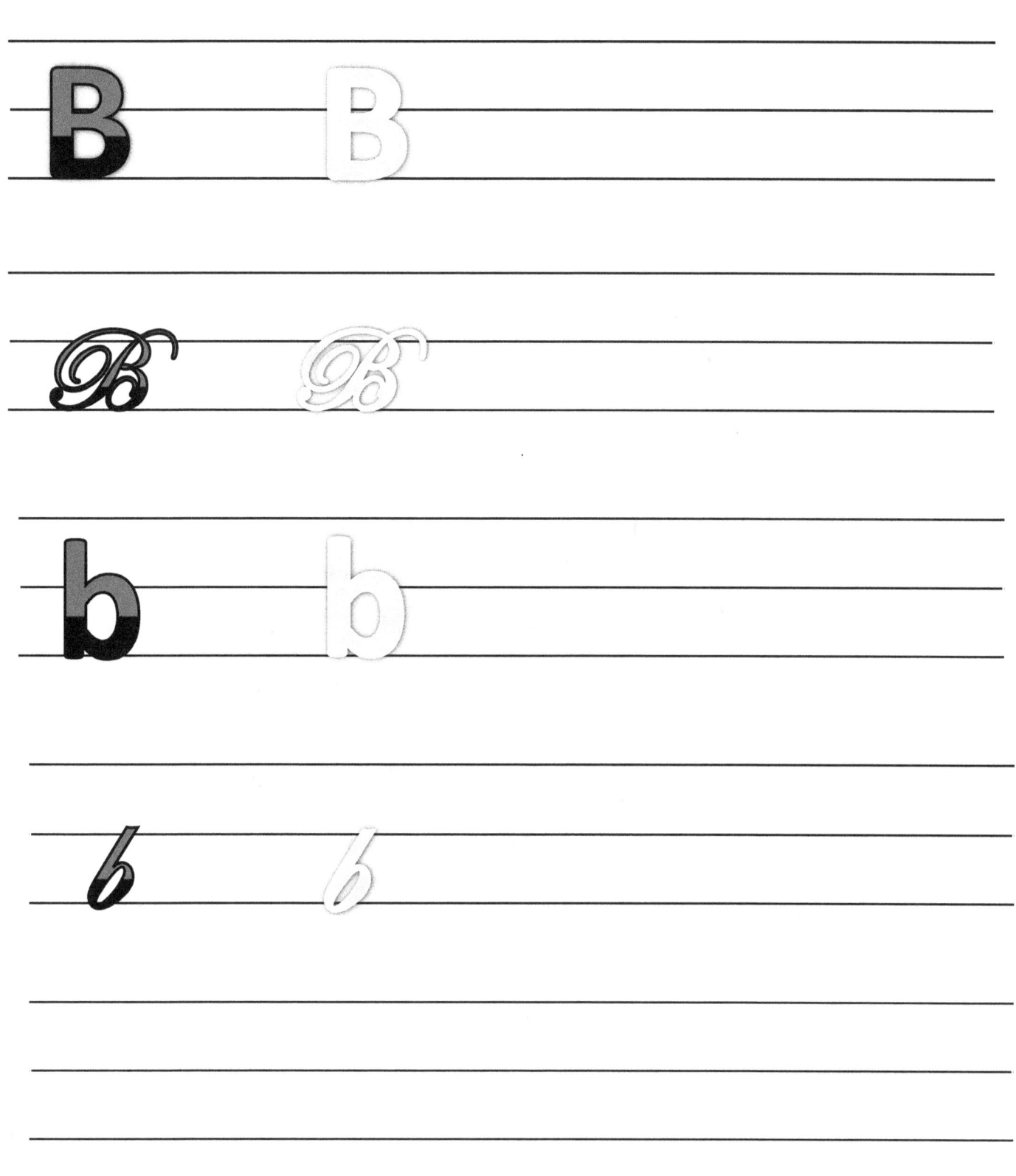

SAY & COLOR

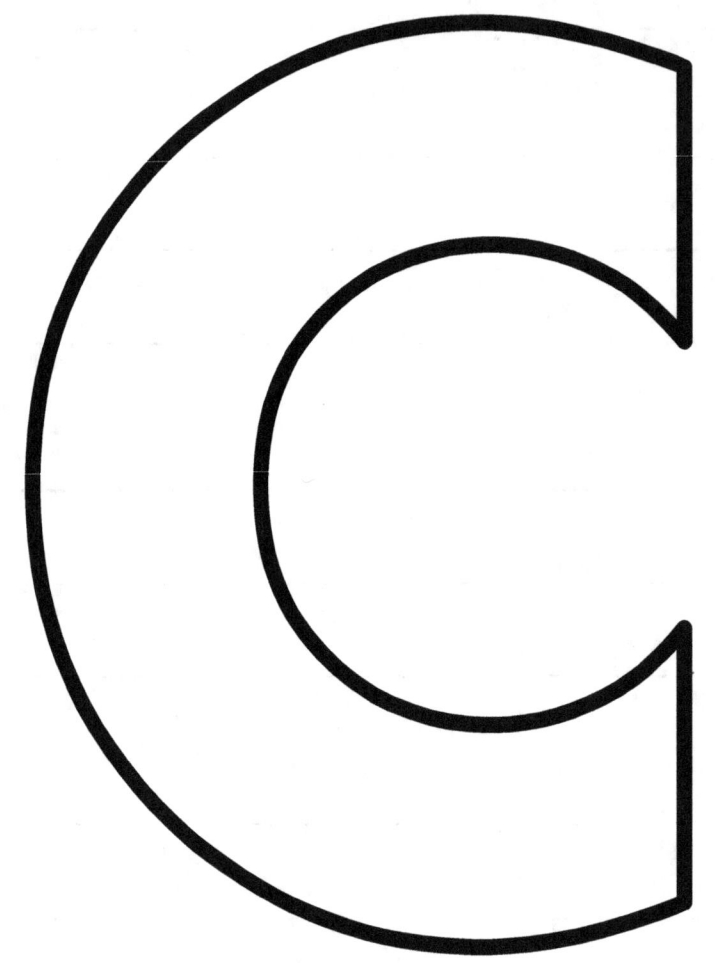

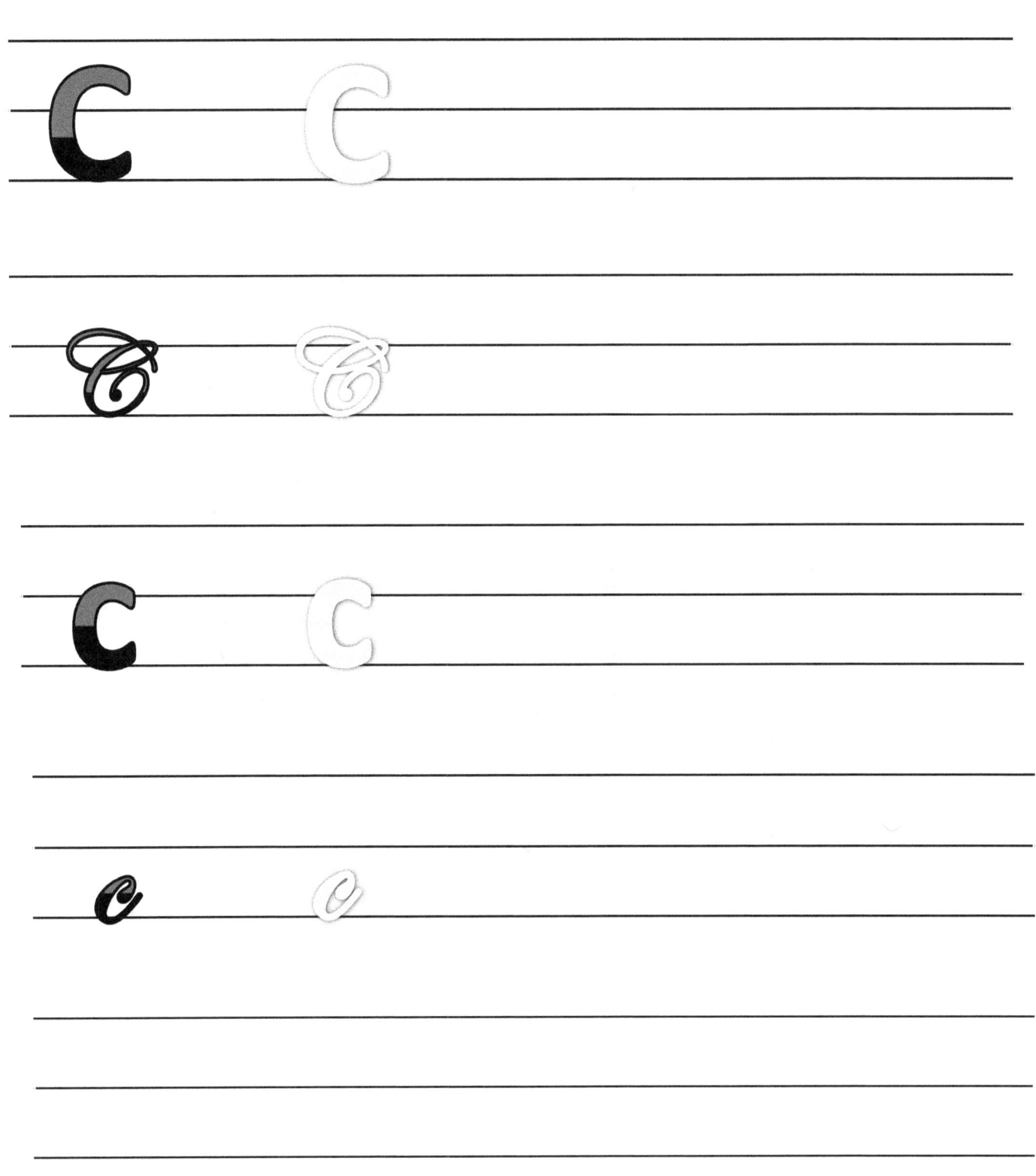

SAY & COLOR

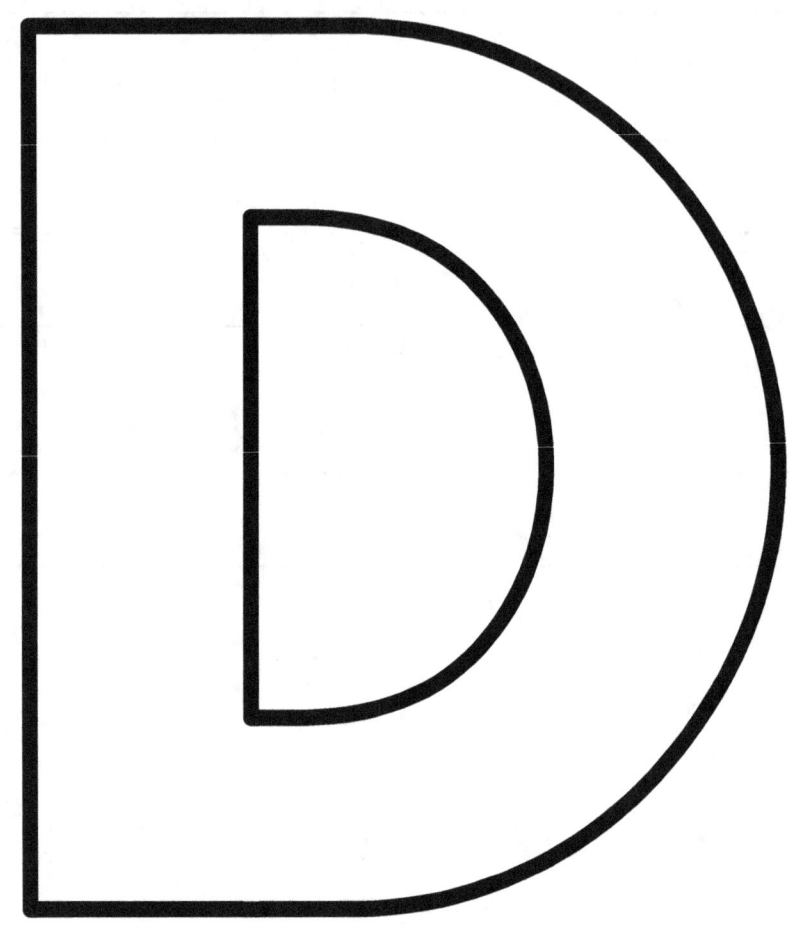

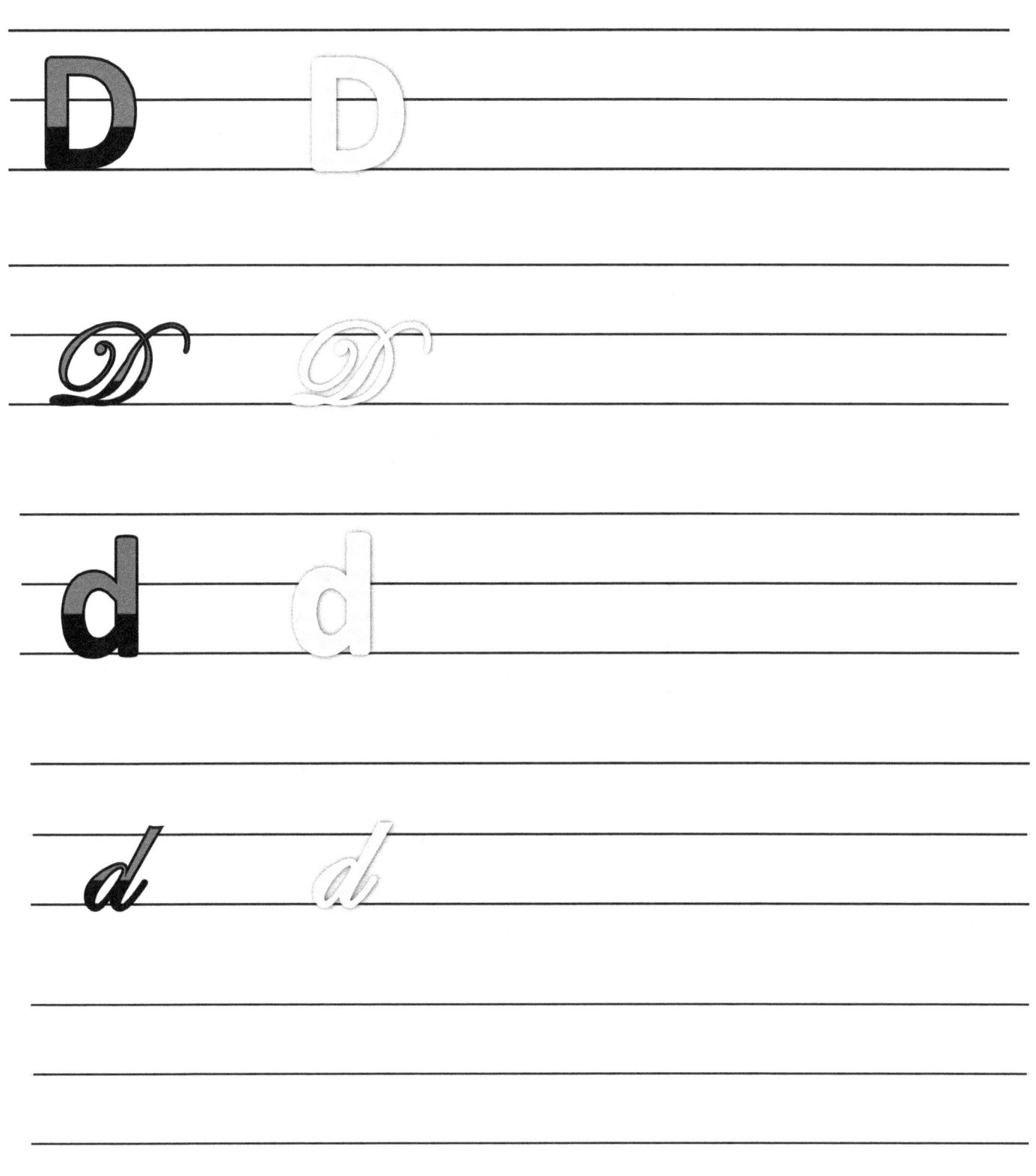

SAY & COLOR

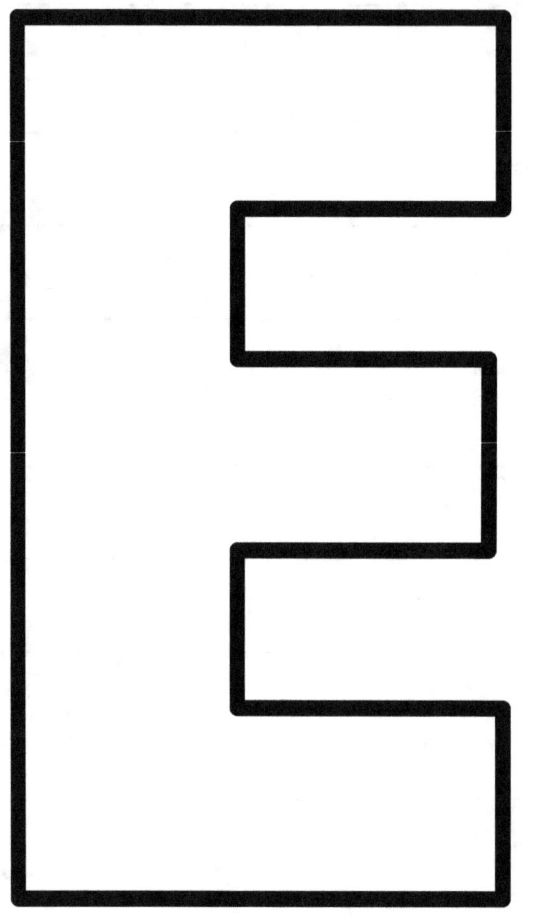

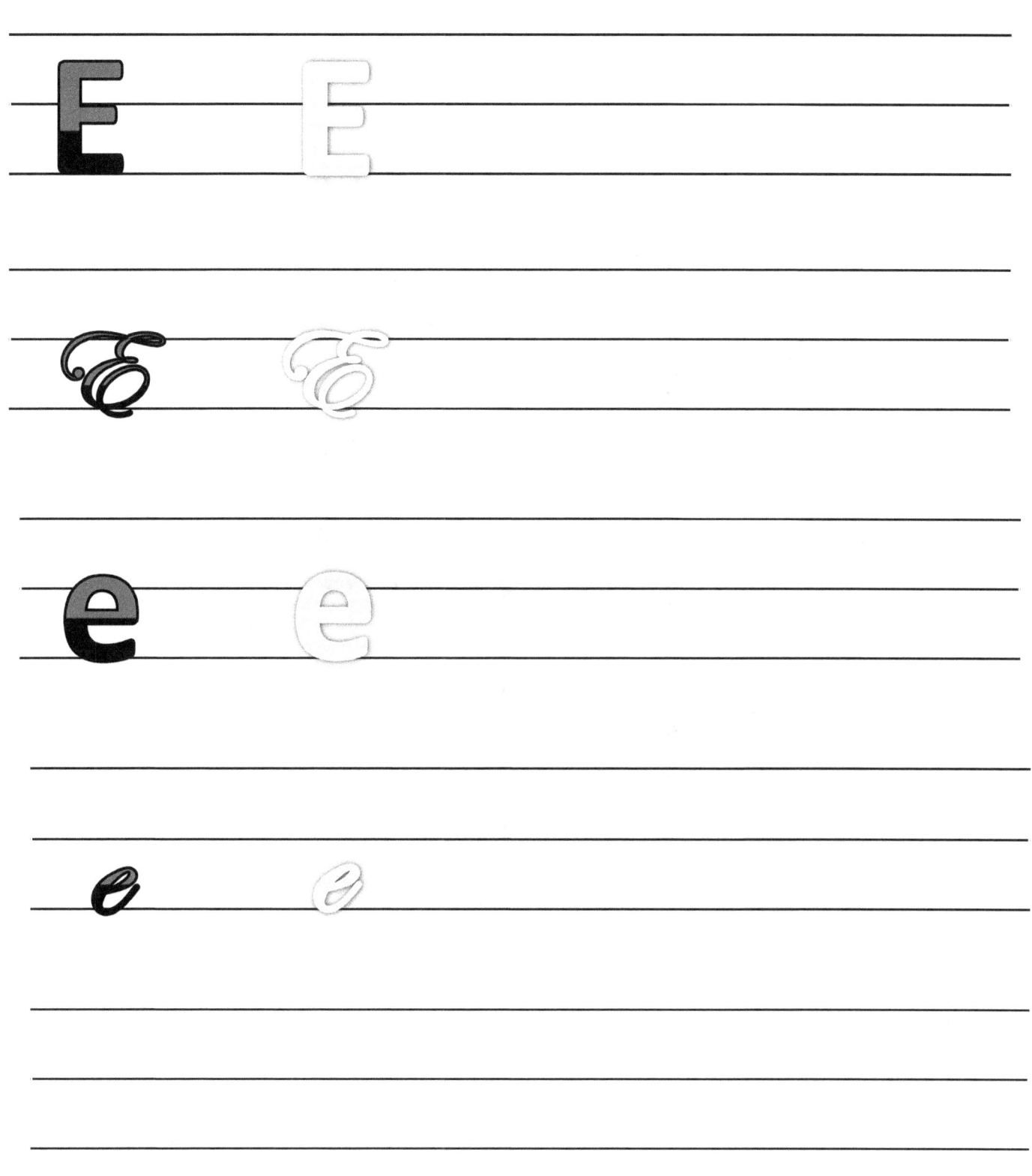

SAY & COLOR

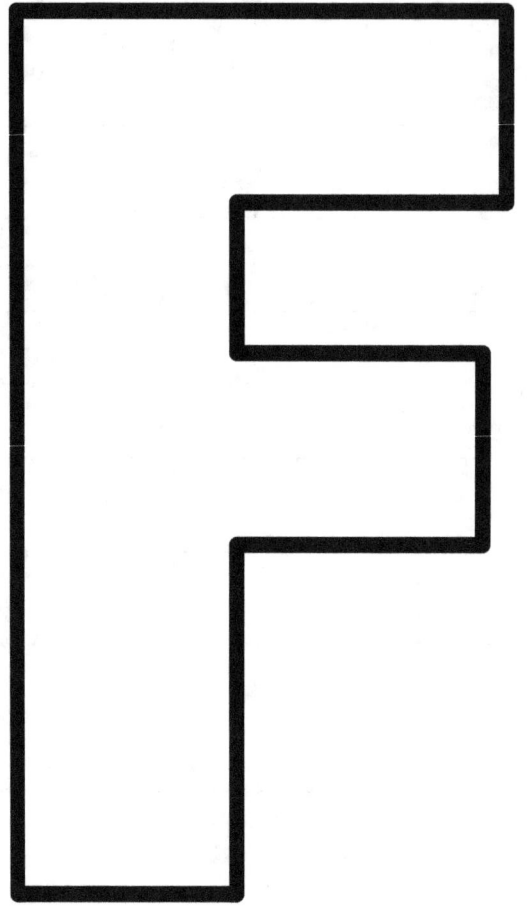

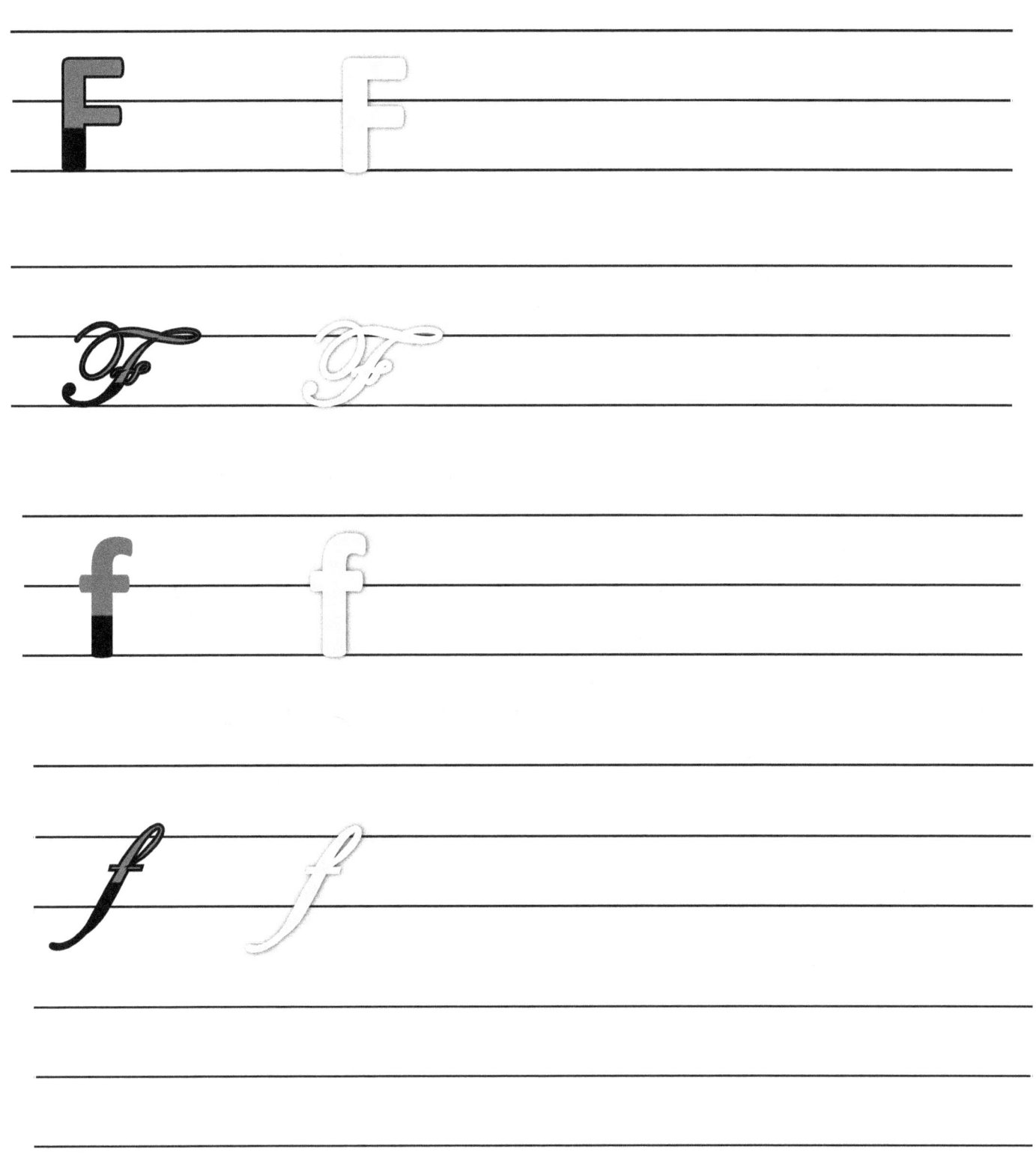

SAY & COLOR

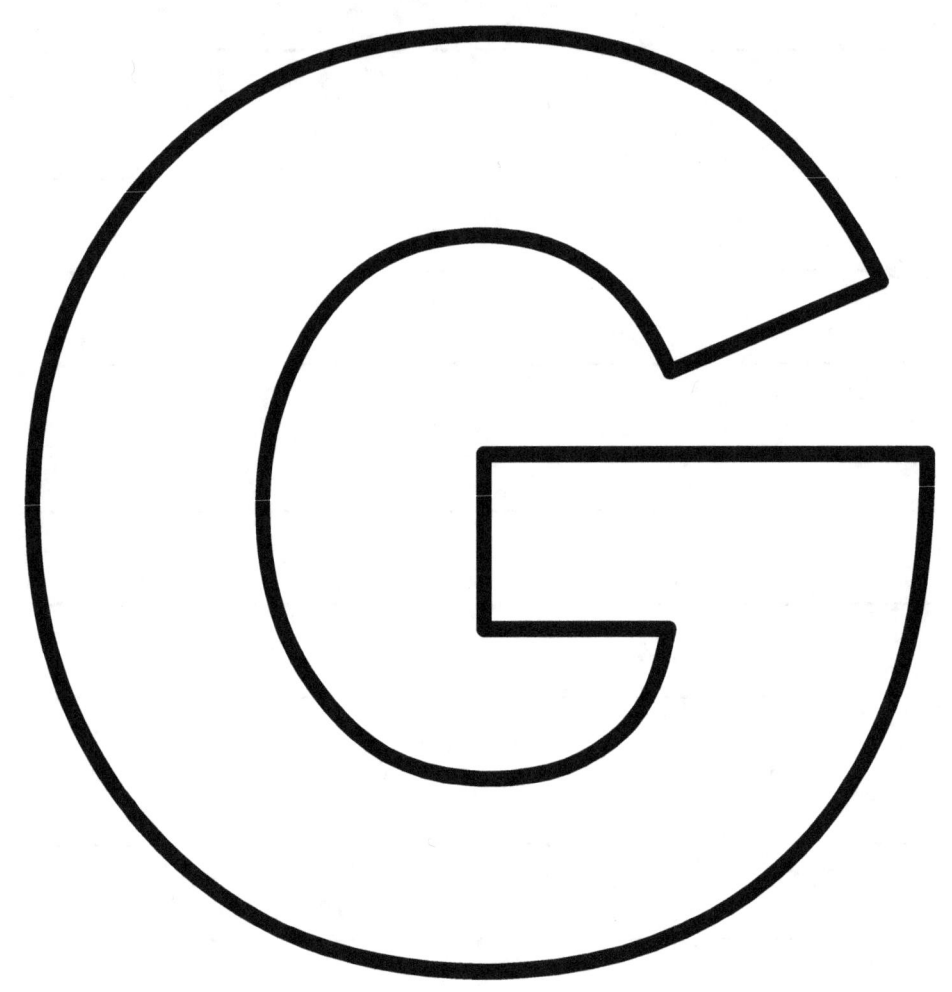

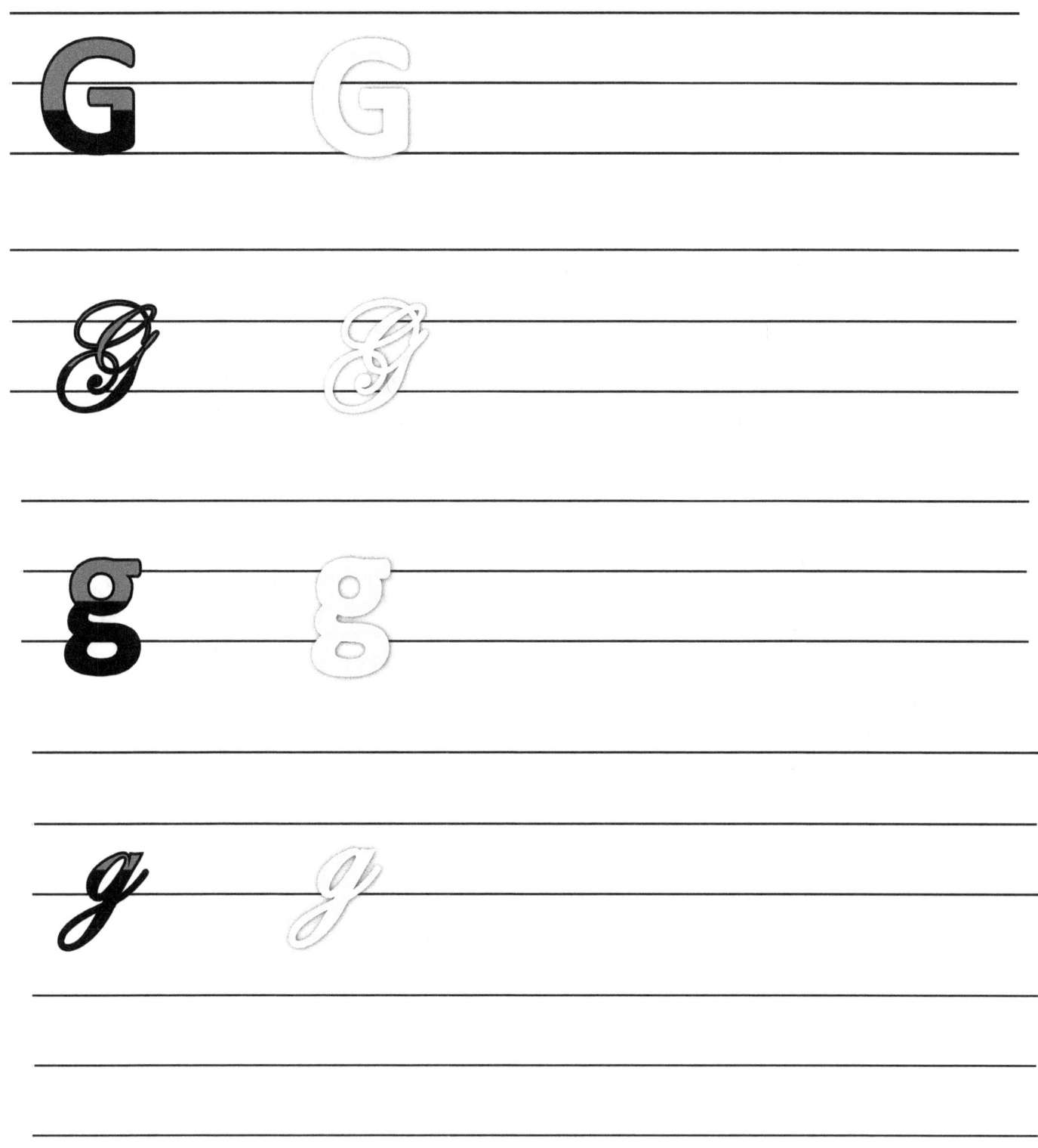

SAY & COLOR

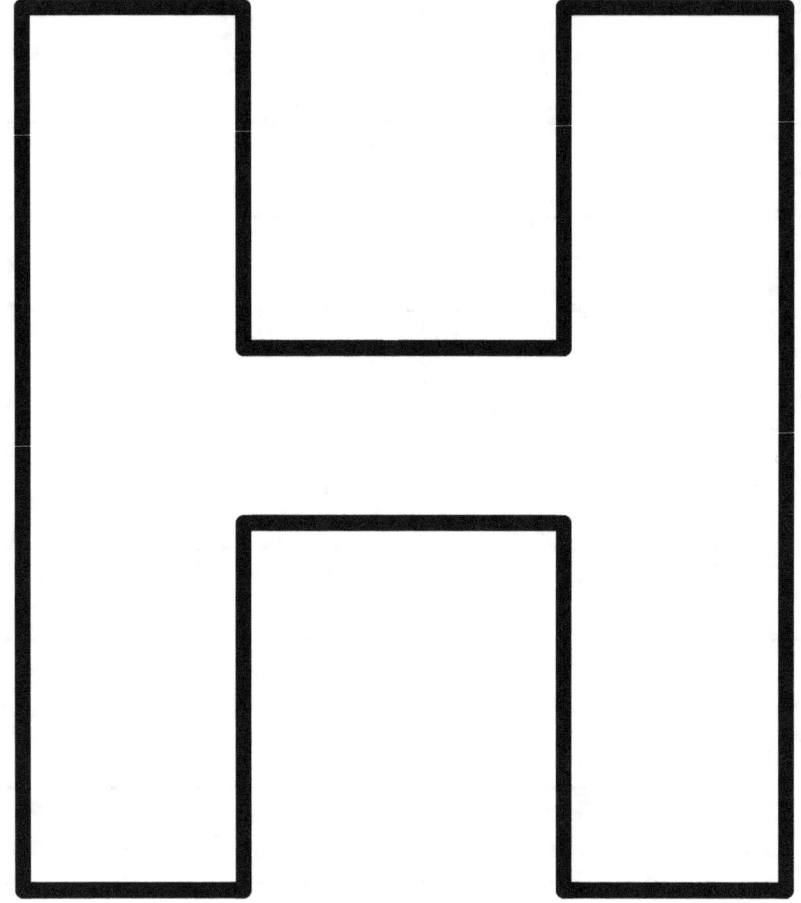

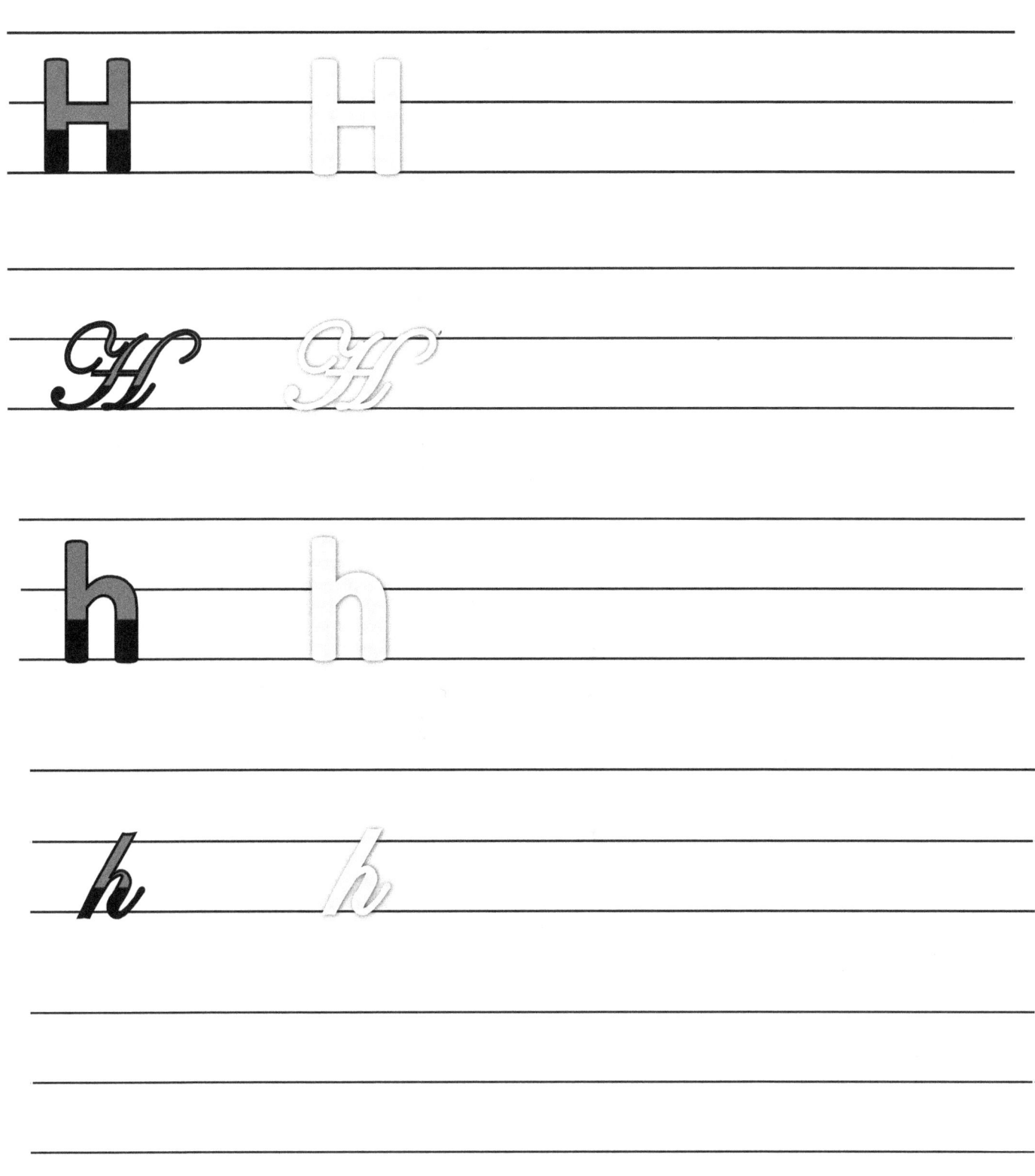

SAY & COLOR

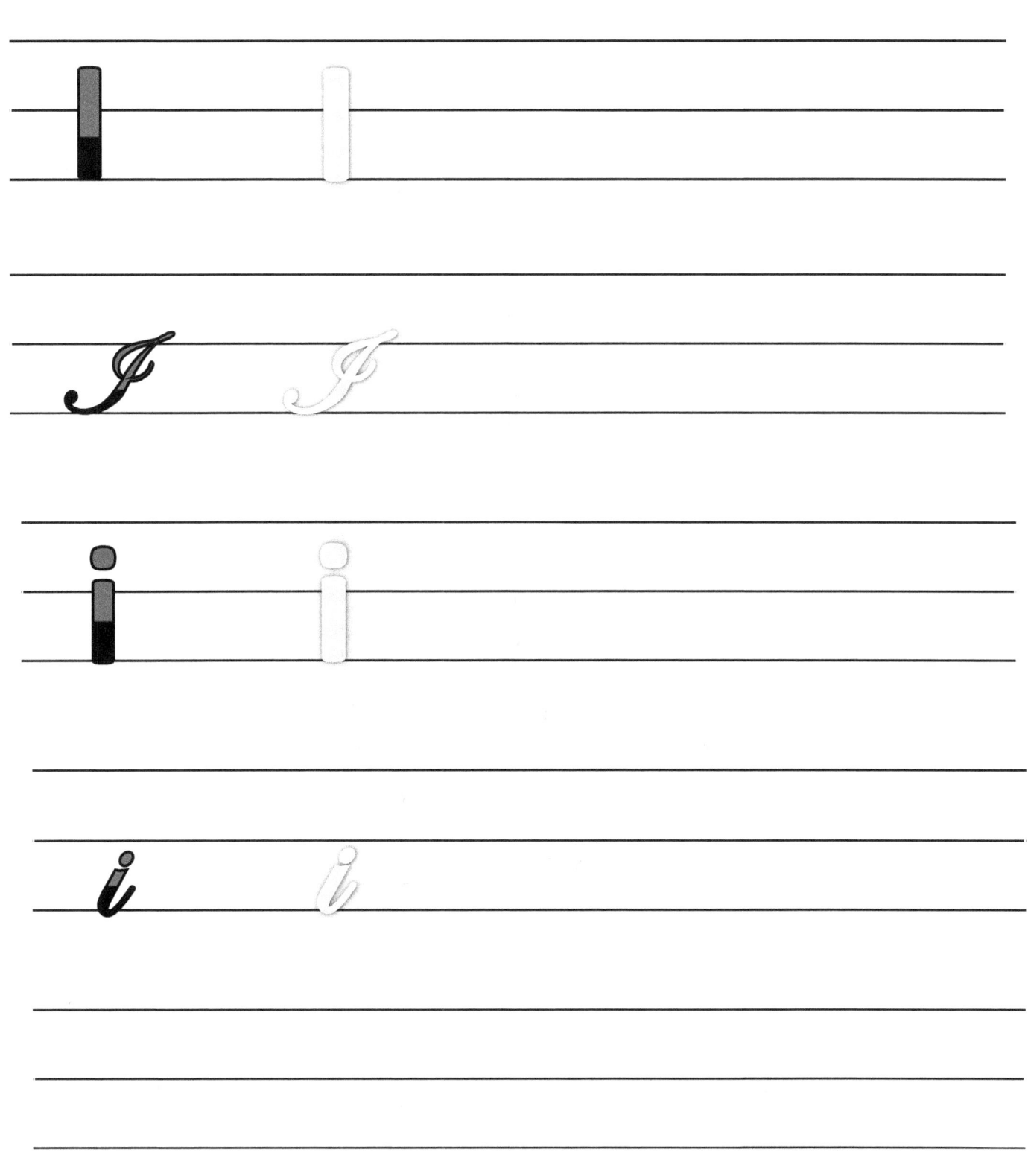

SAY & COLOR

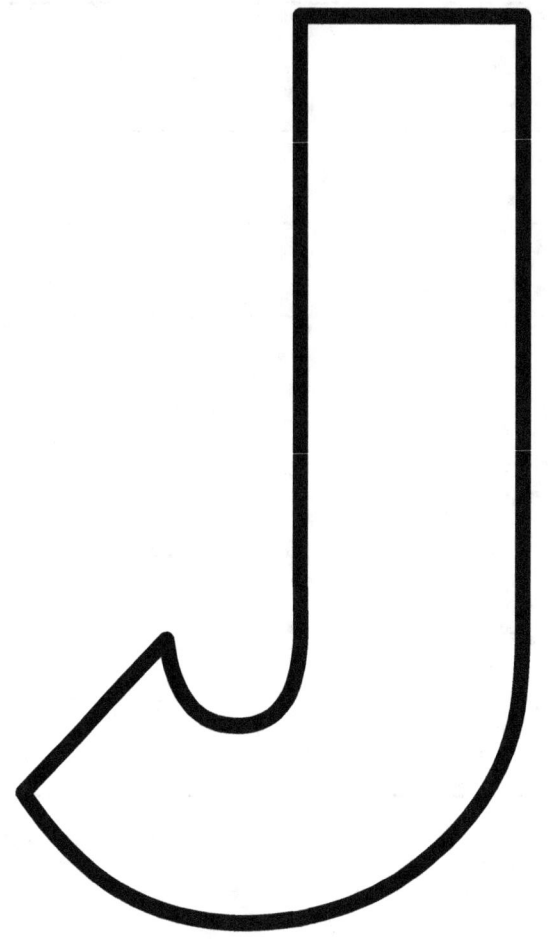

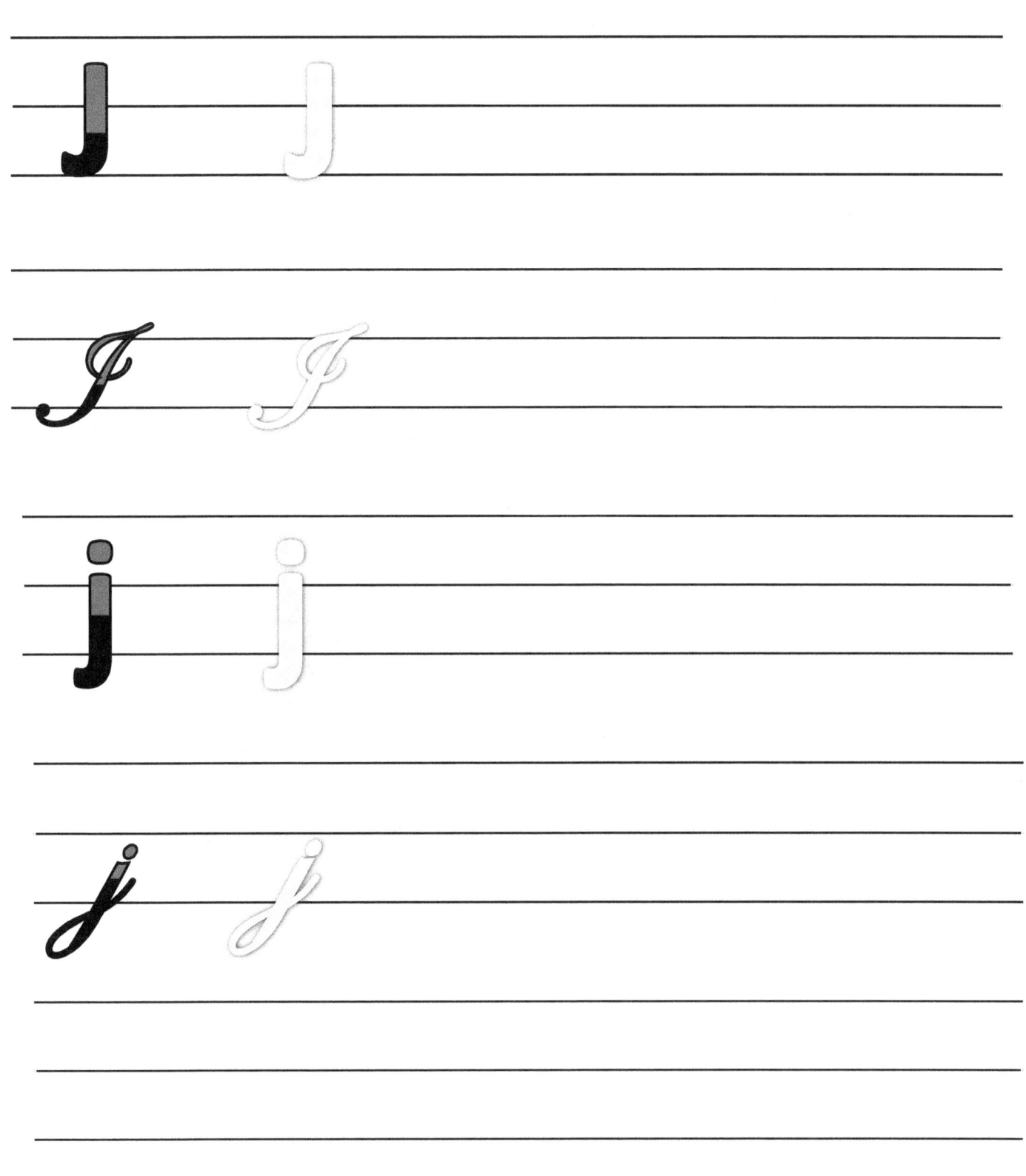

SAY & COLOR

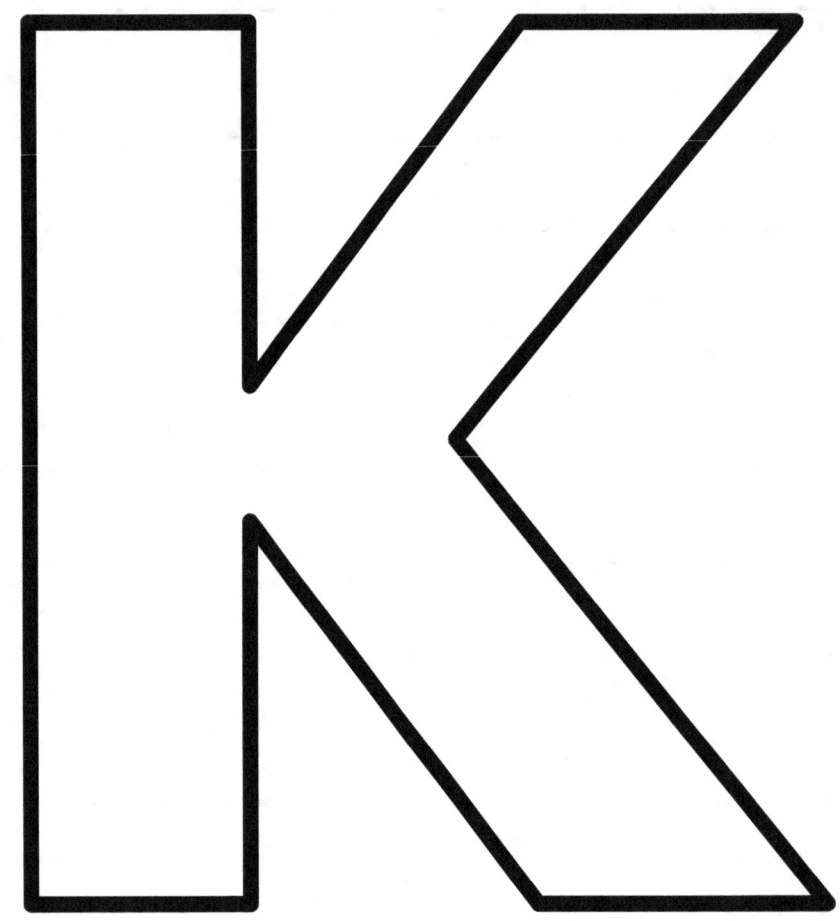

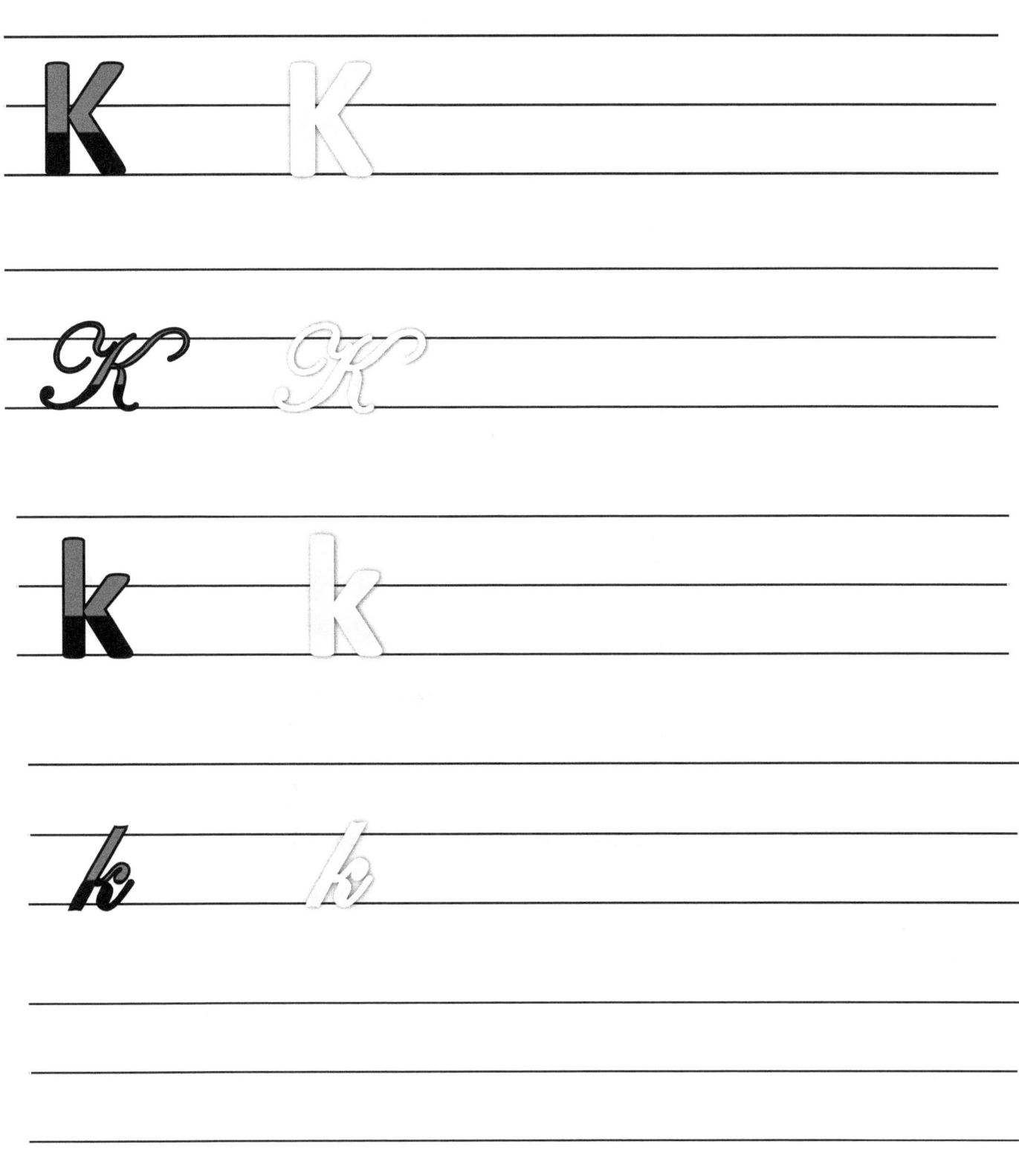

SAY & COLOR

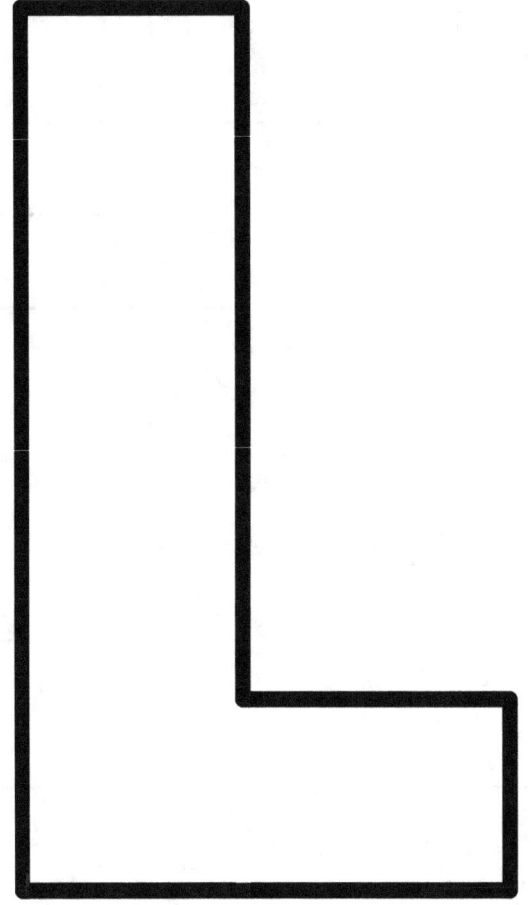

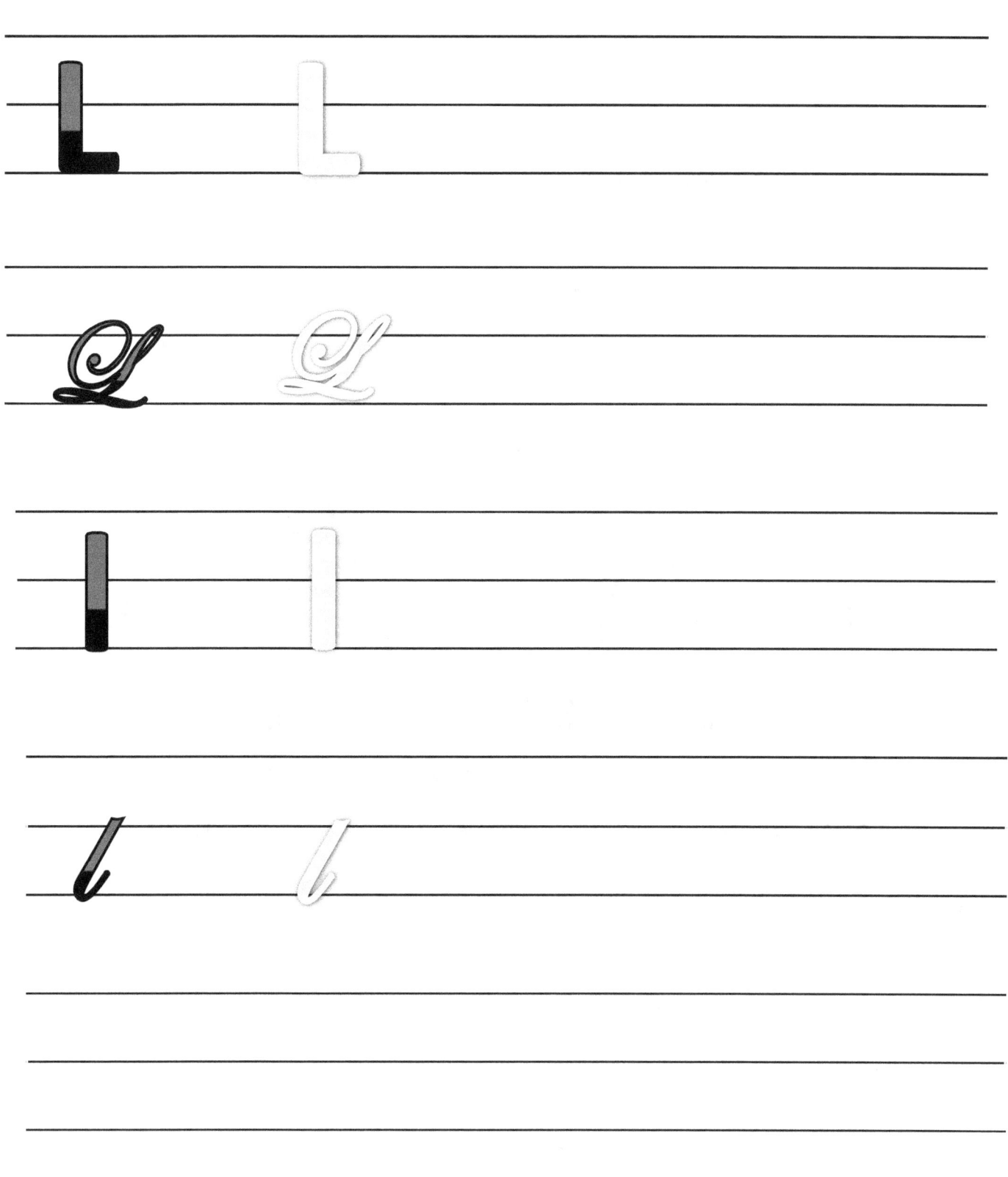

SAY & COLOR

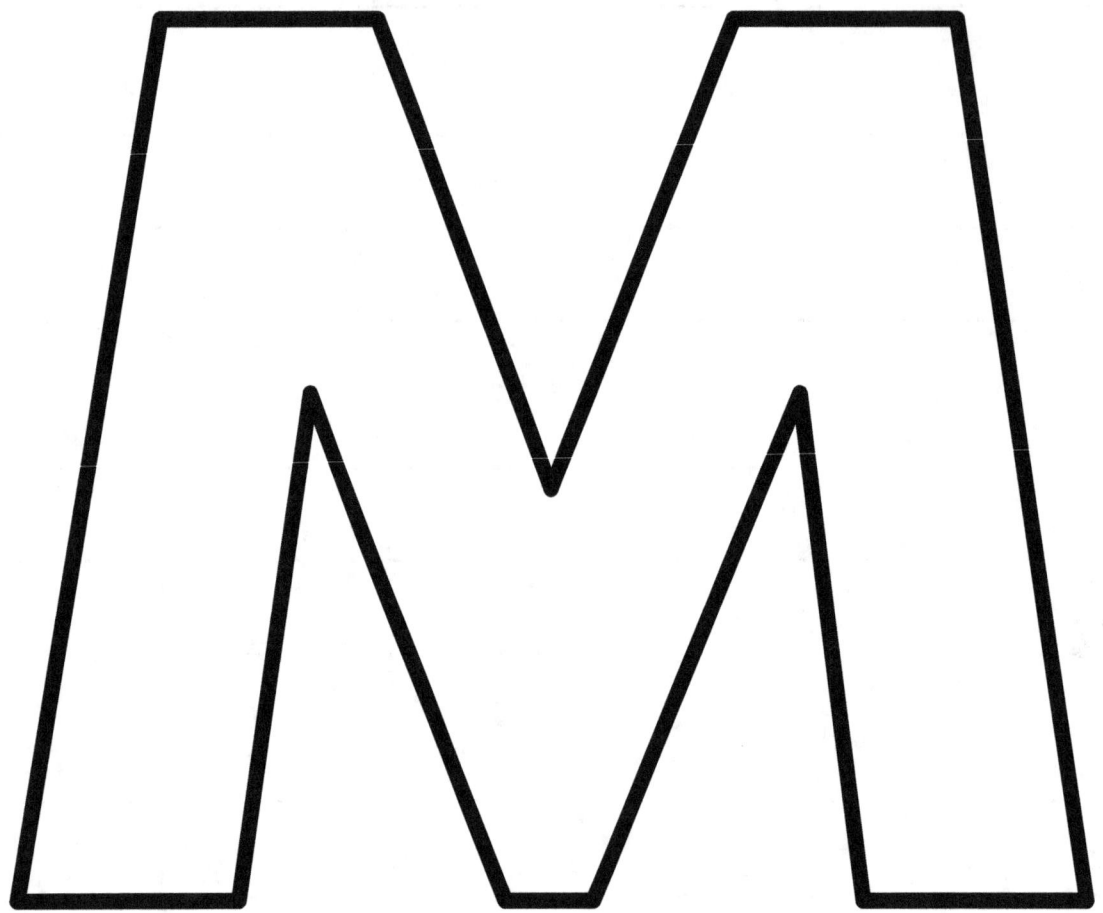

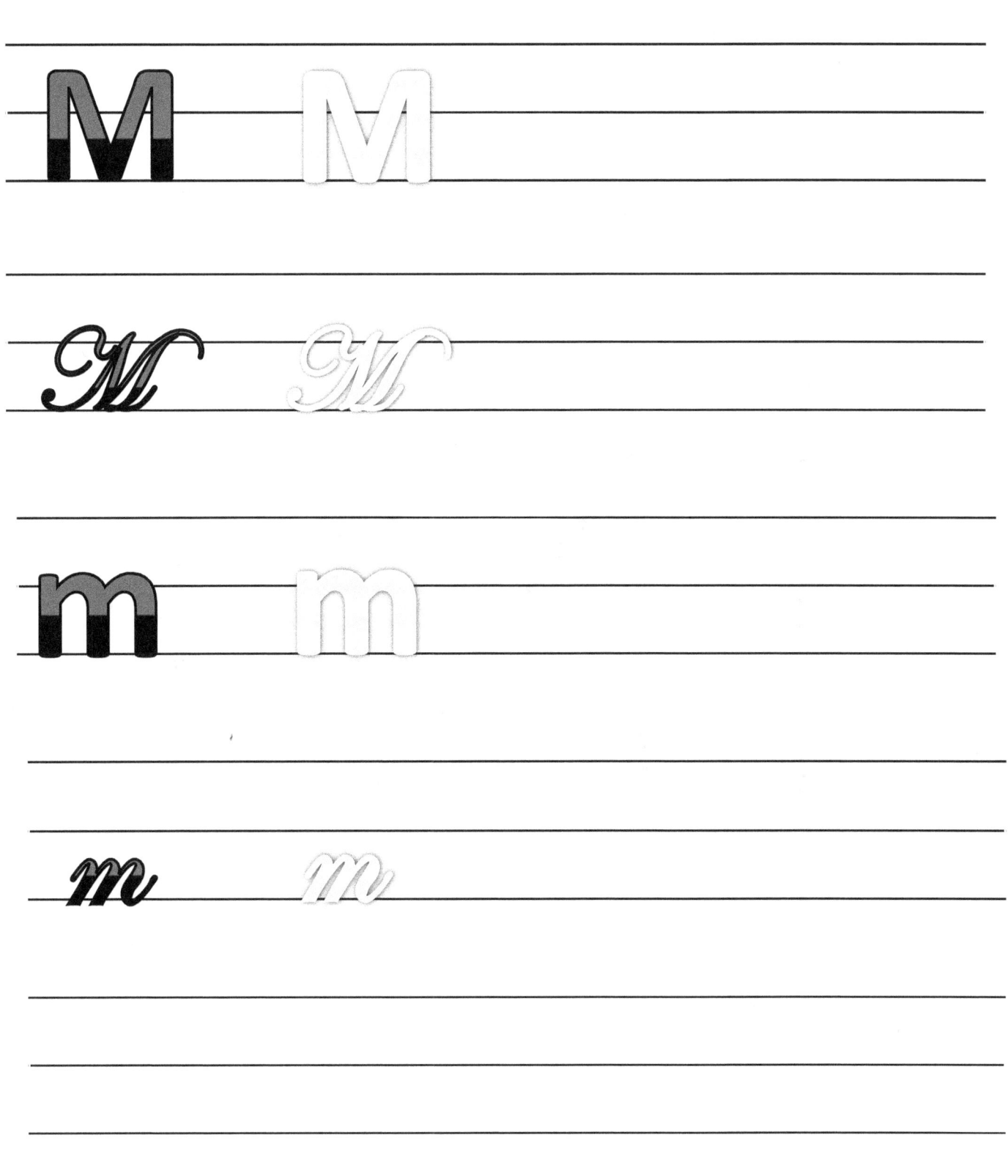

SAY & COLOR

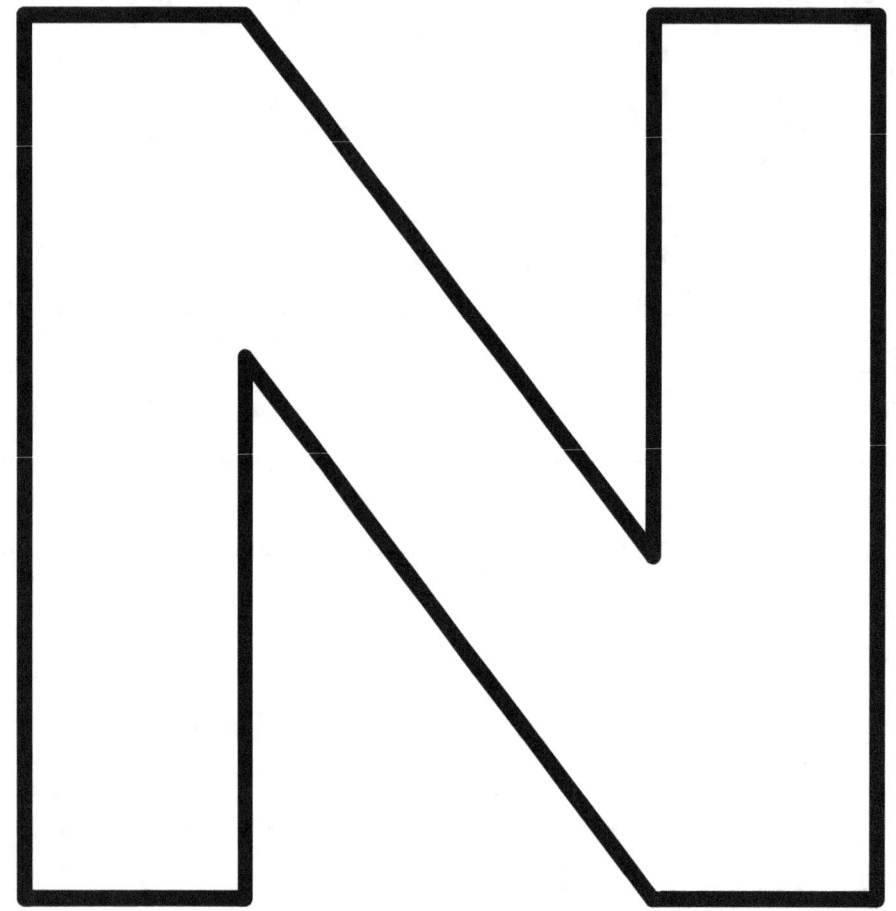

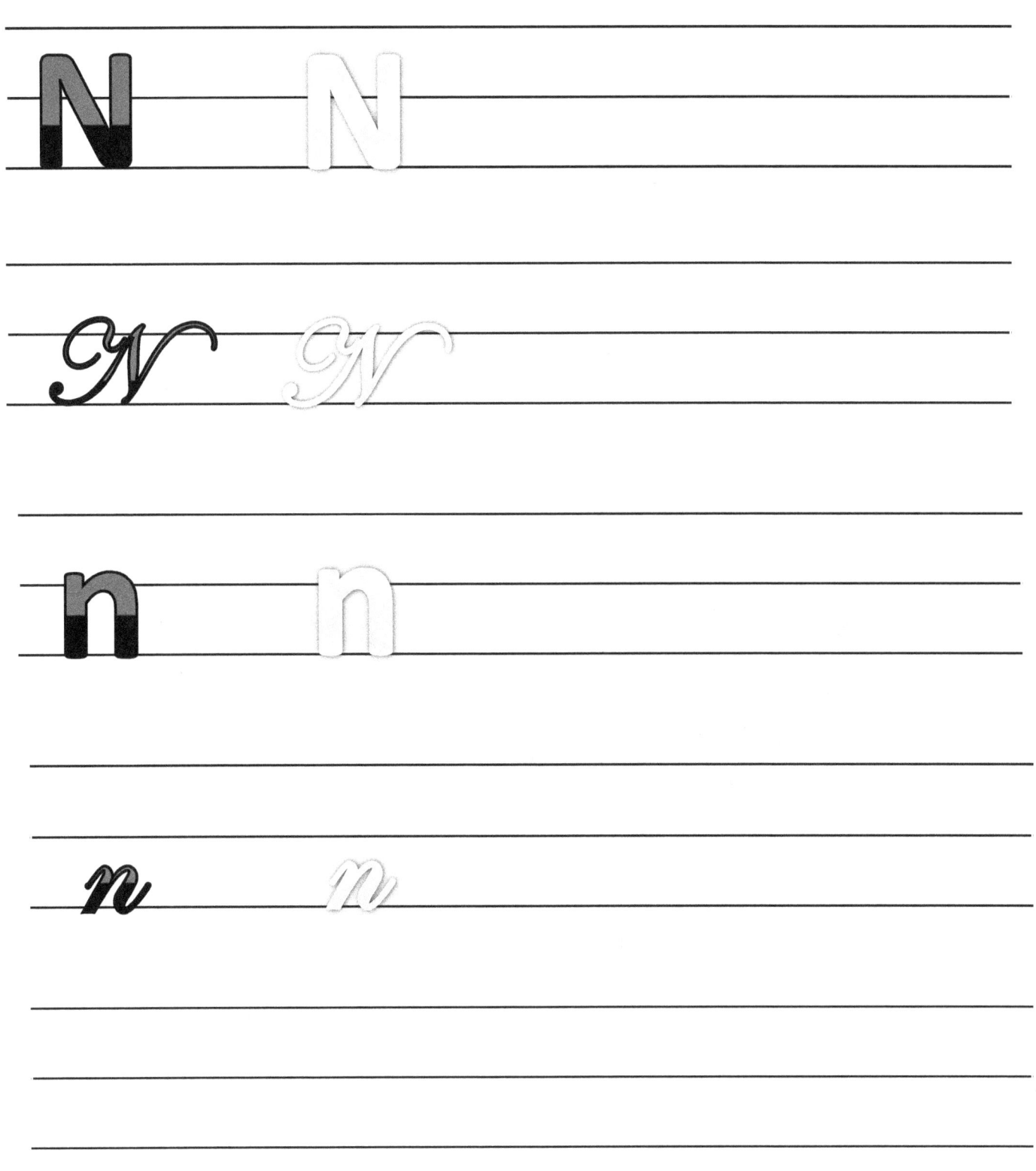

SAY & COLOR

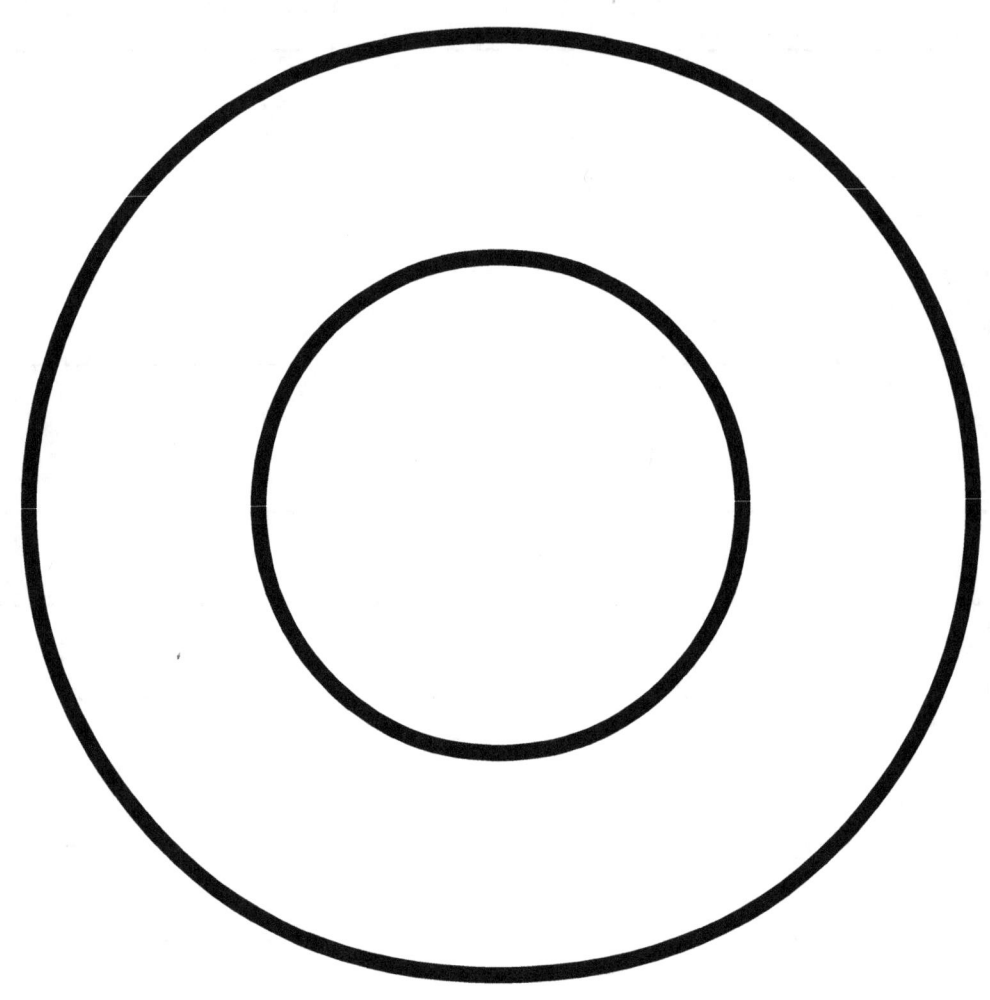

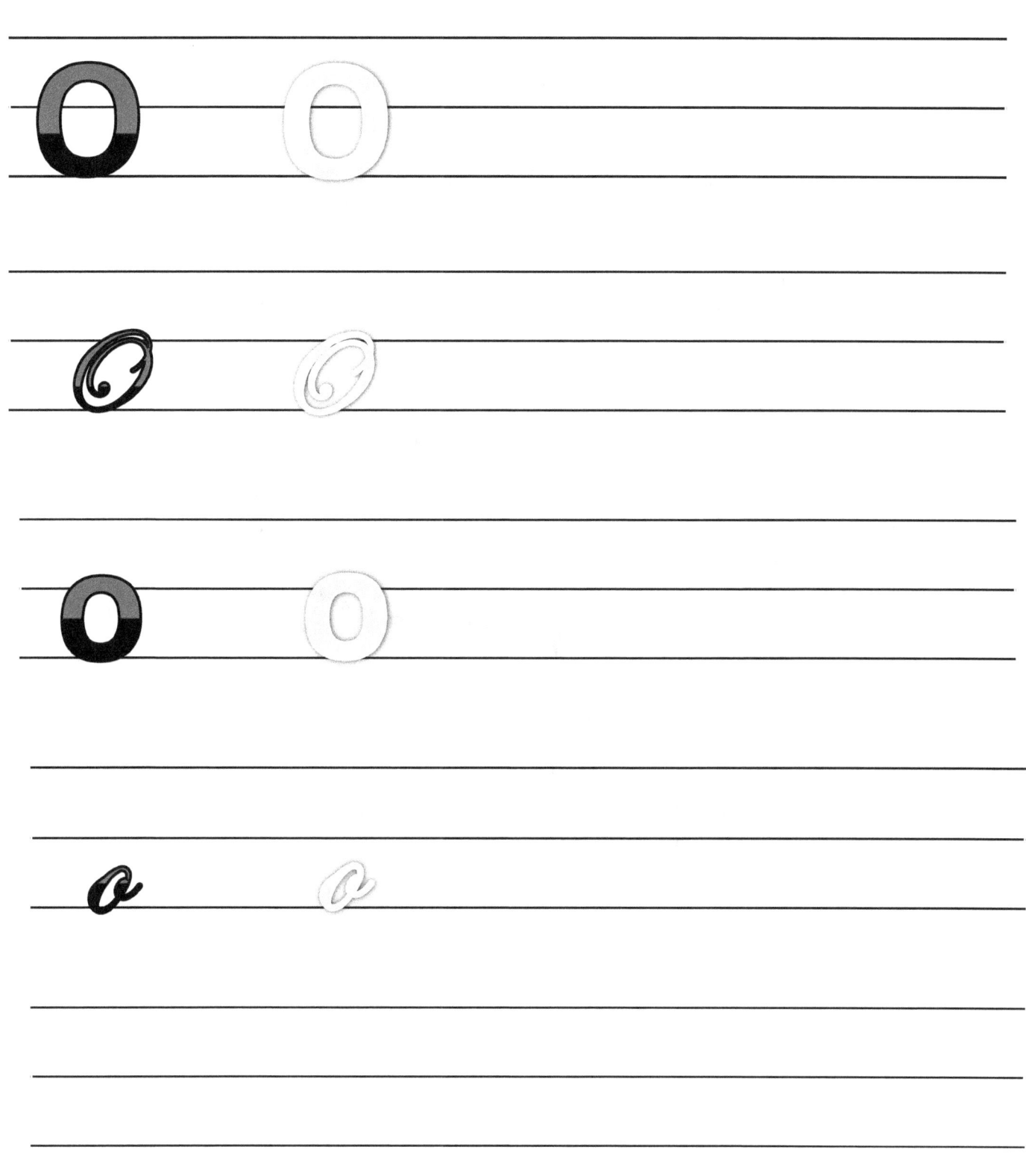

SAY & COLOR

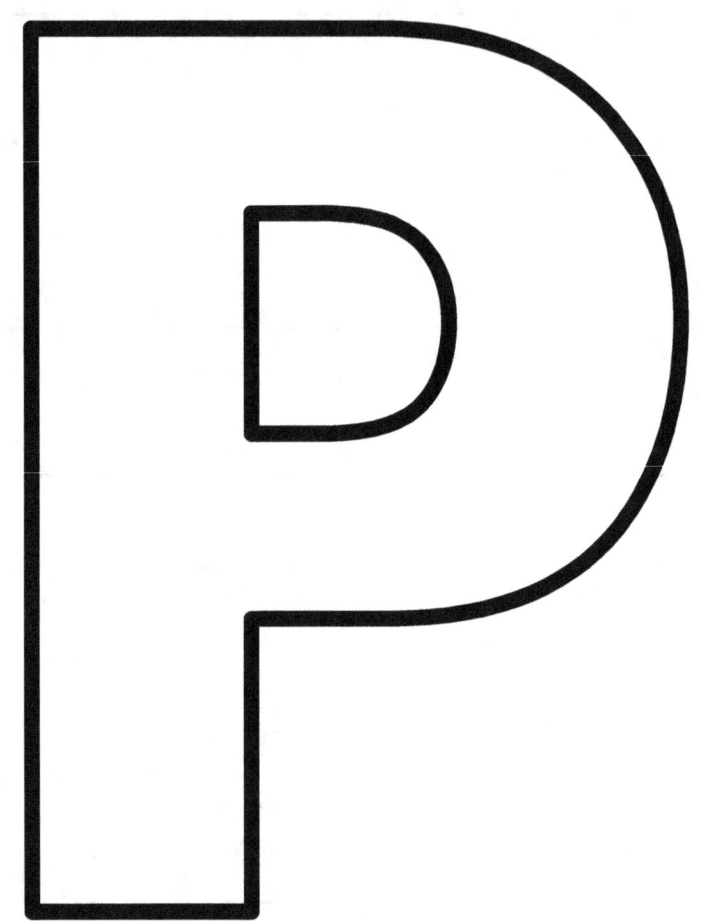

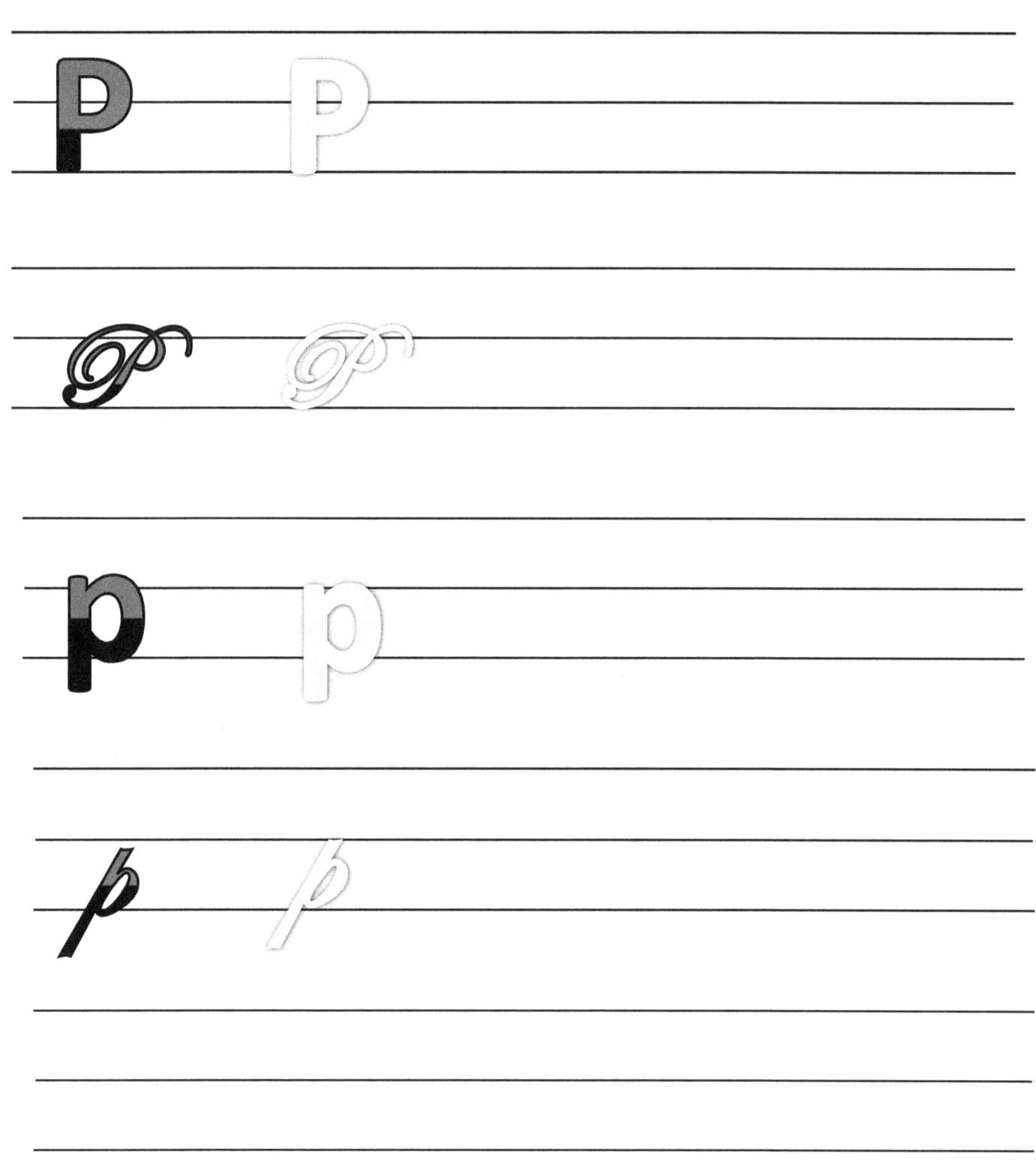

SAY & COLOR

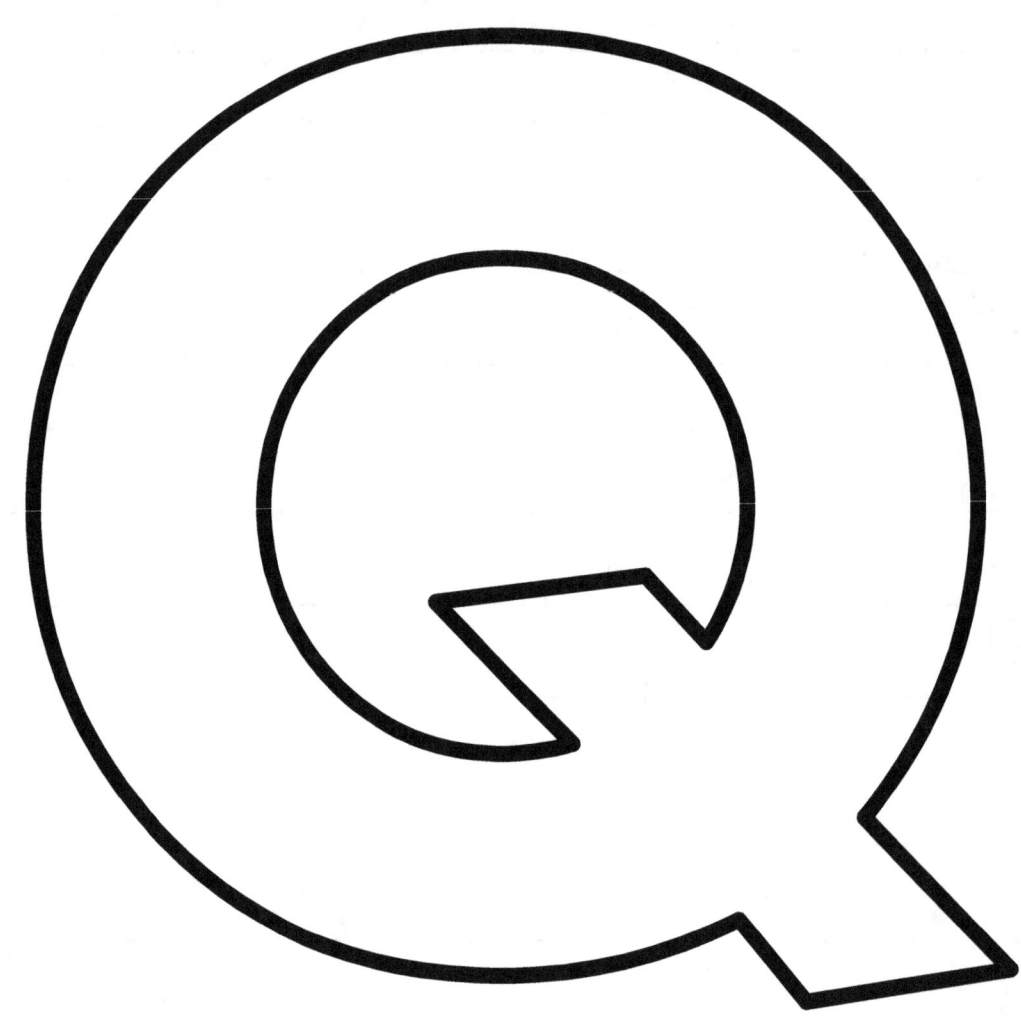

SAY & COLOR

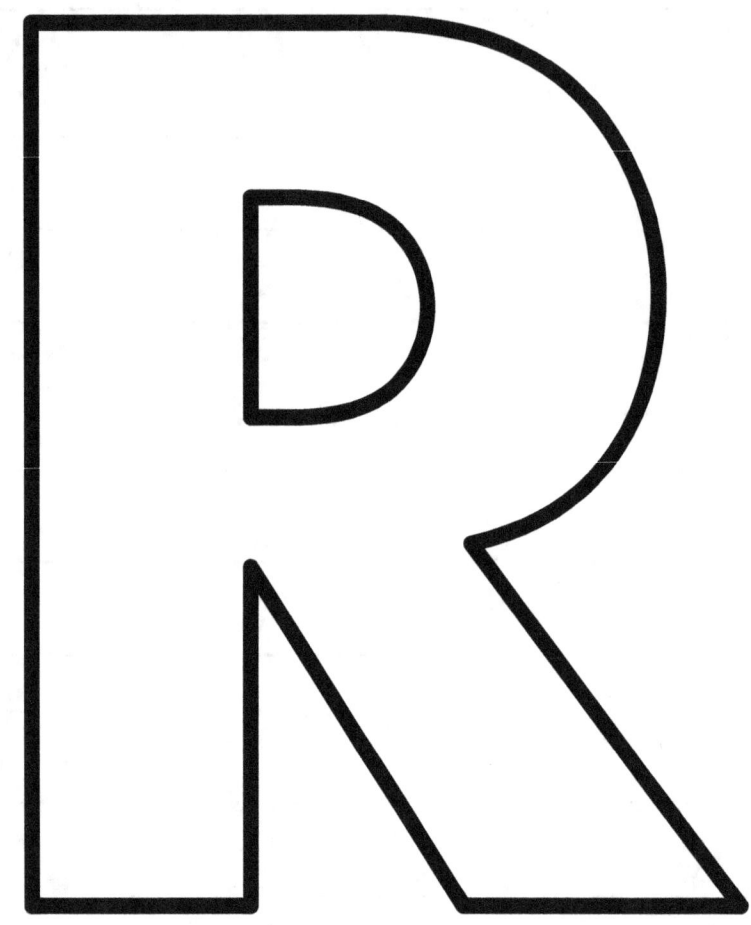

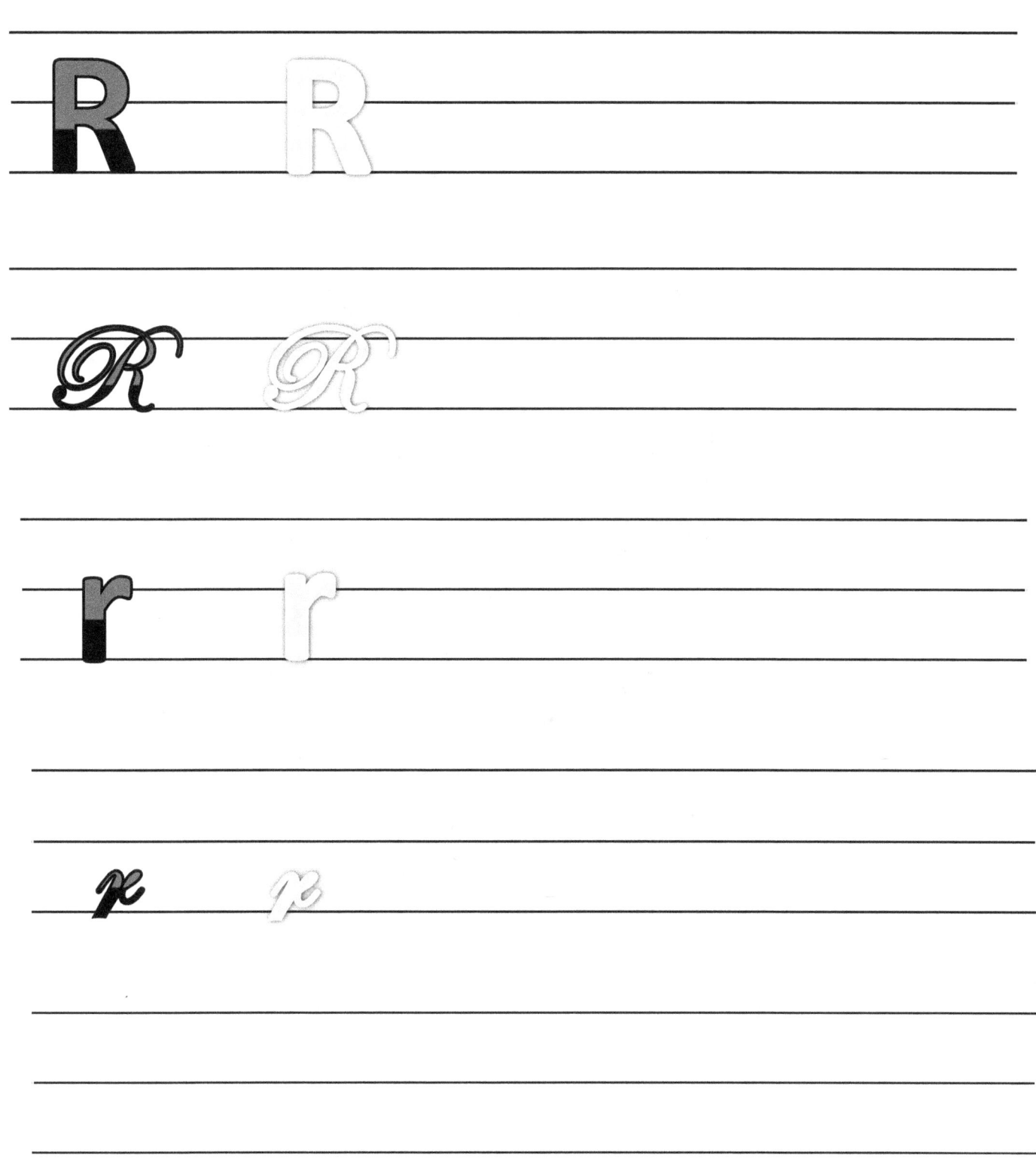

SAY & COLOR

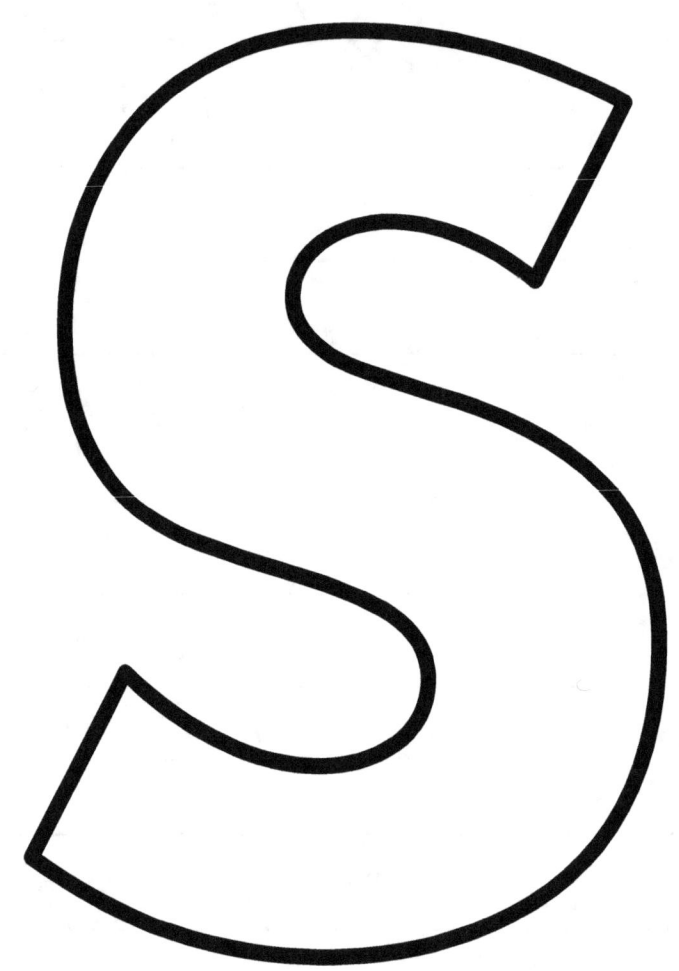

S S

𝒮 𝒮

S S

𝒔 𝒔

SAY & COLOR

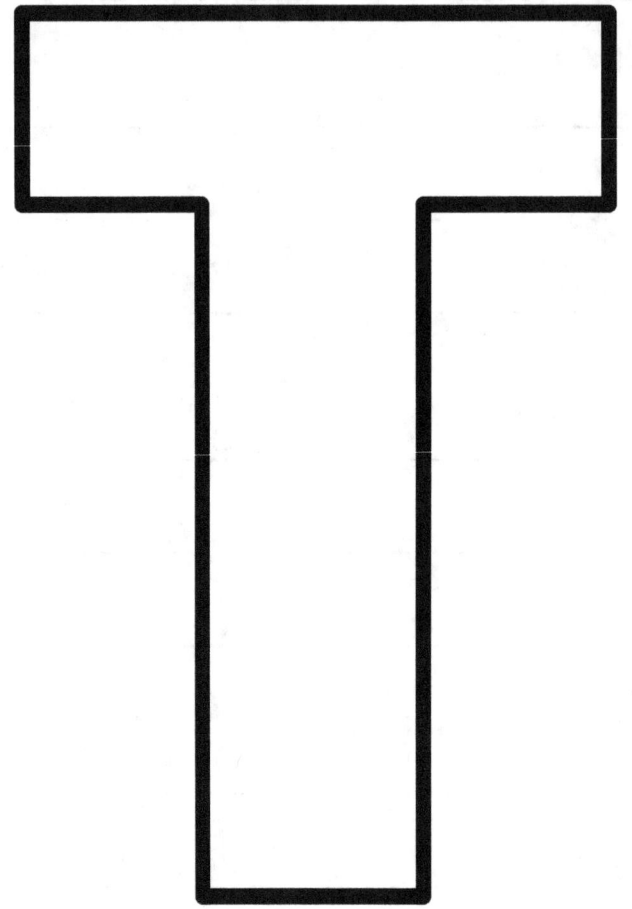

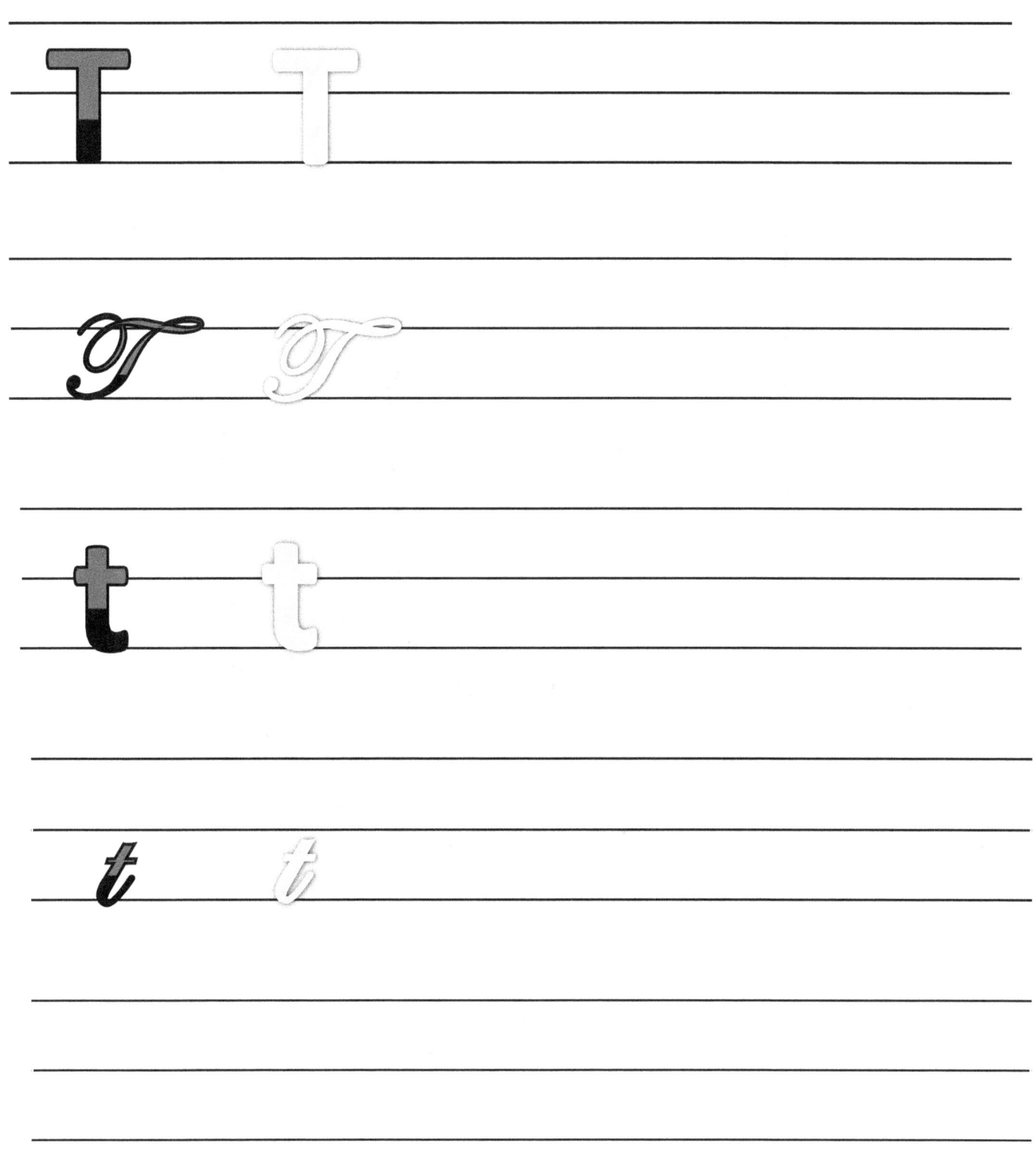

SAY & COLOR

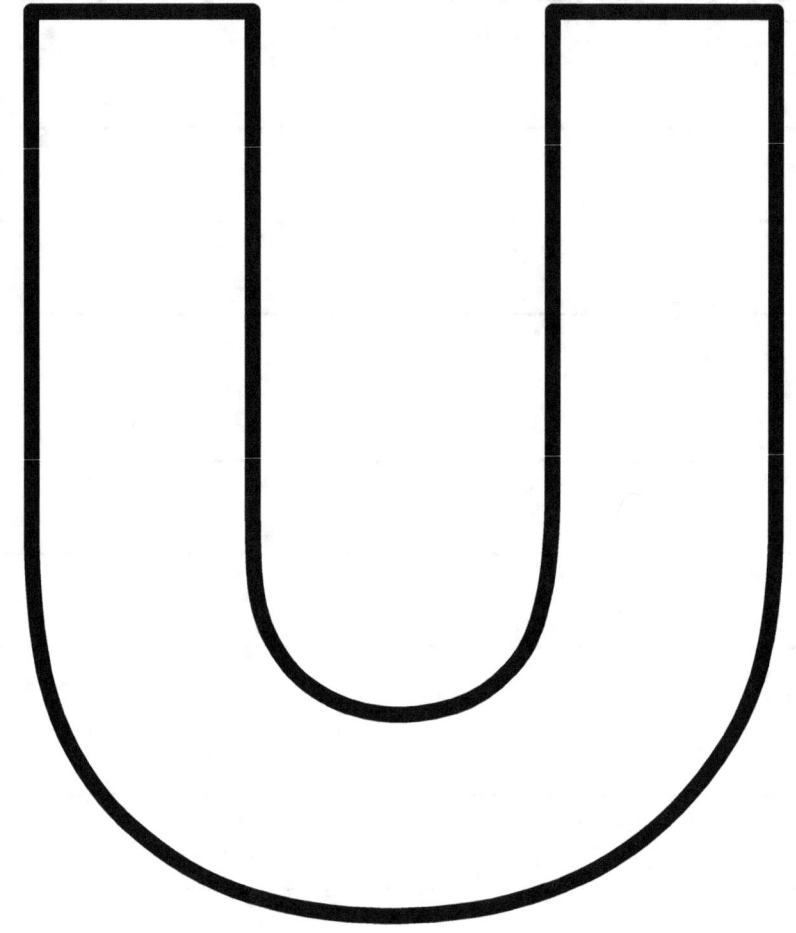

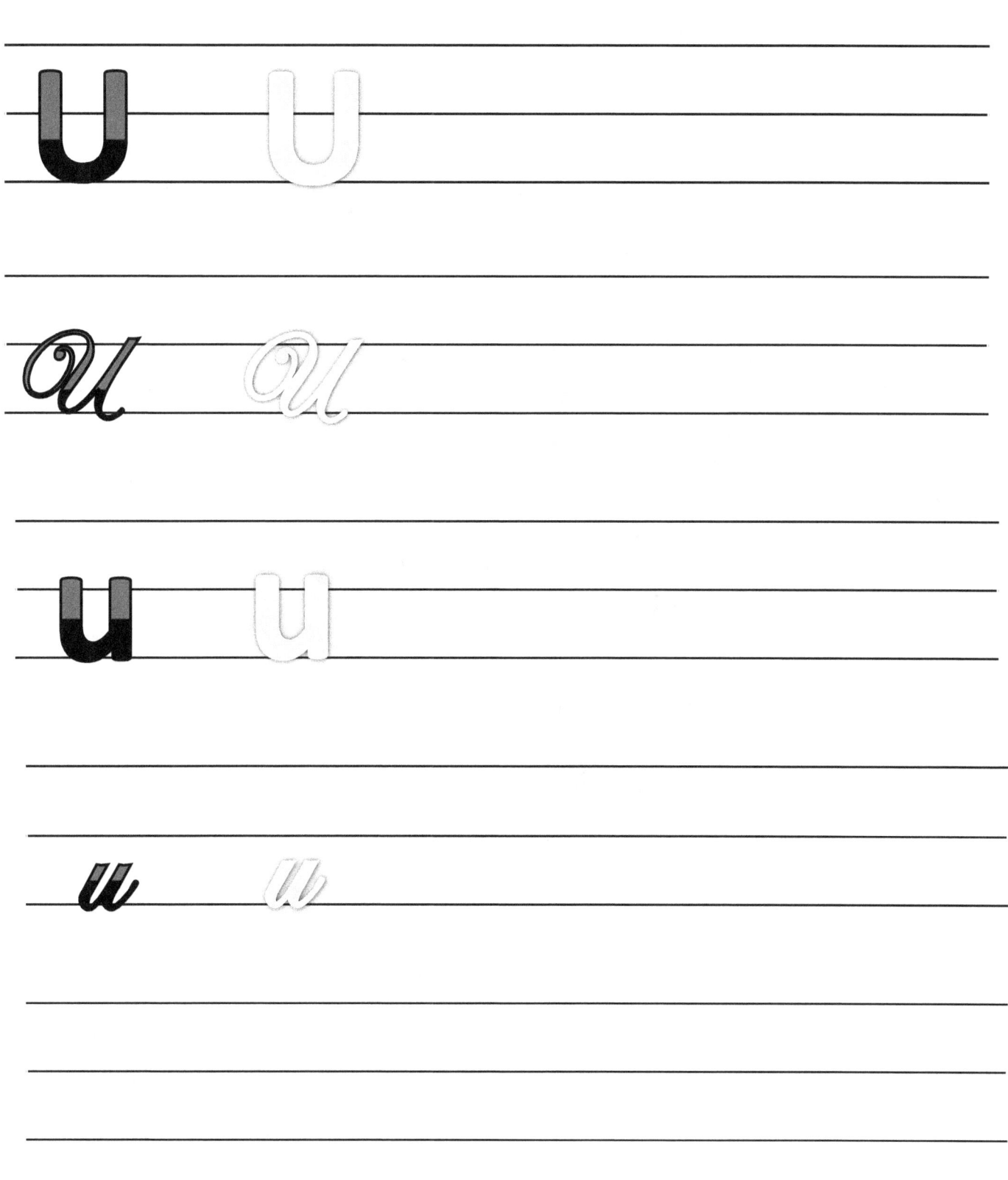

SAY & COLOR

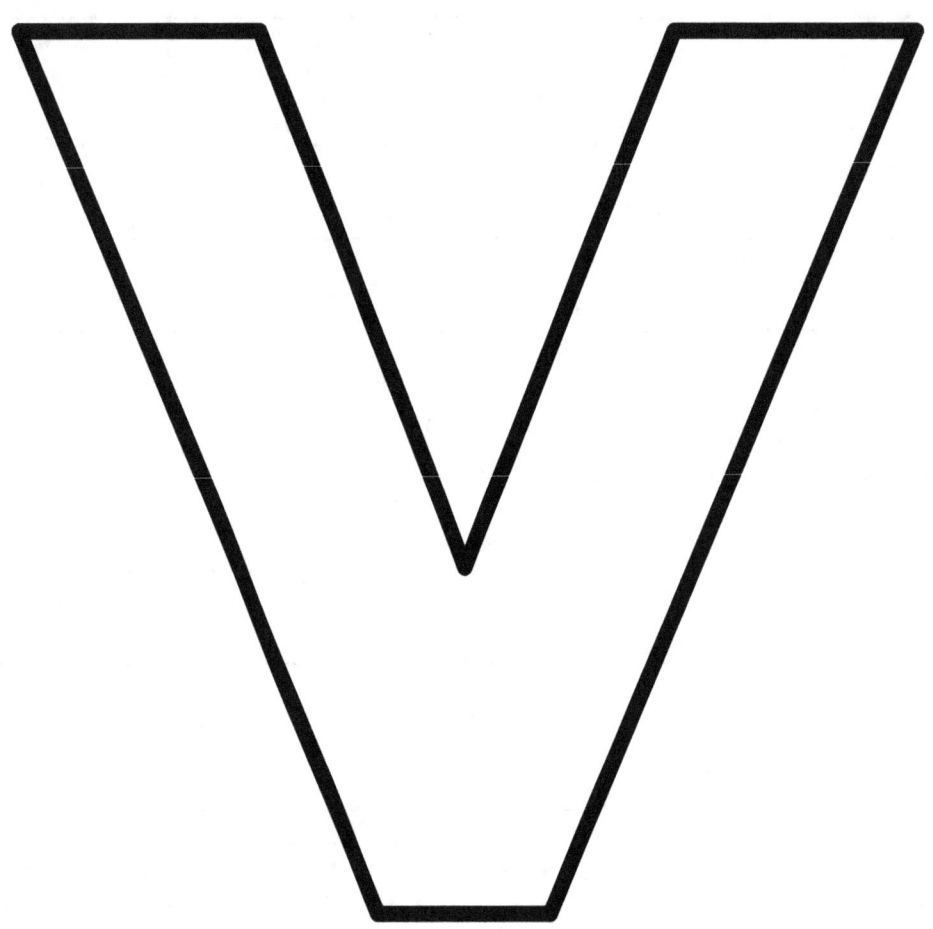

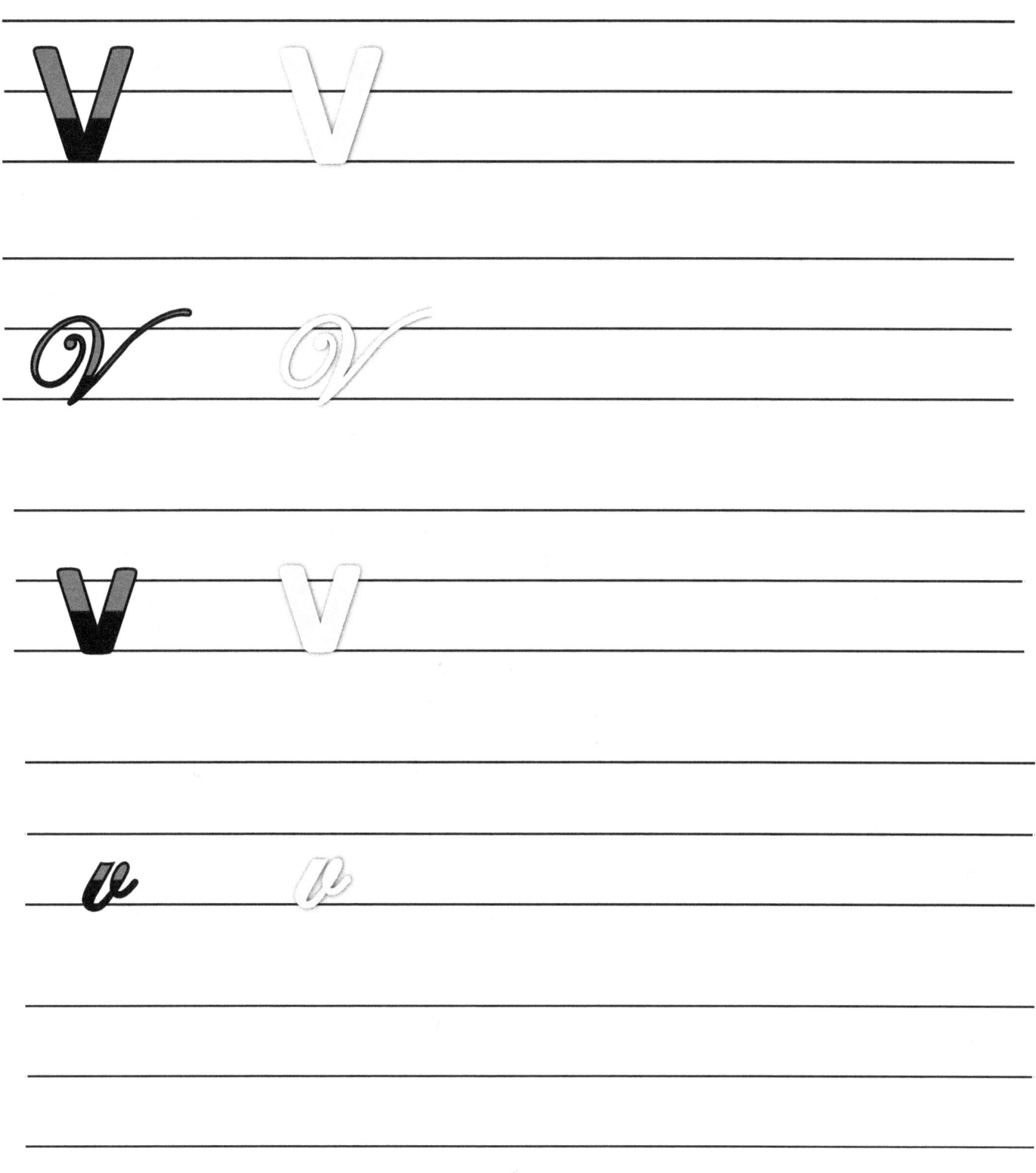

SAY & COLOR

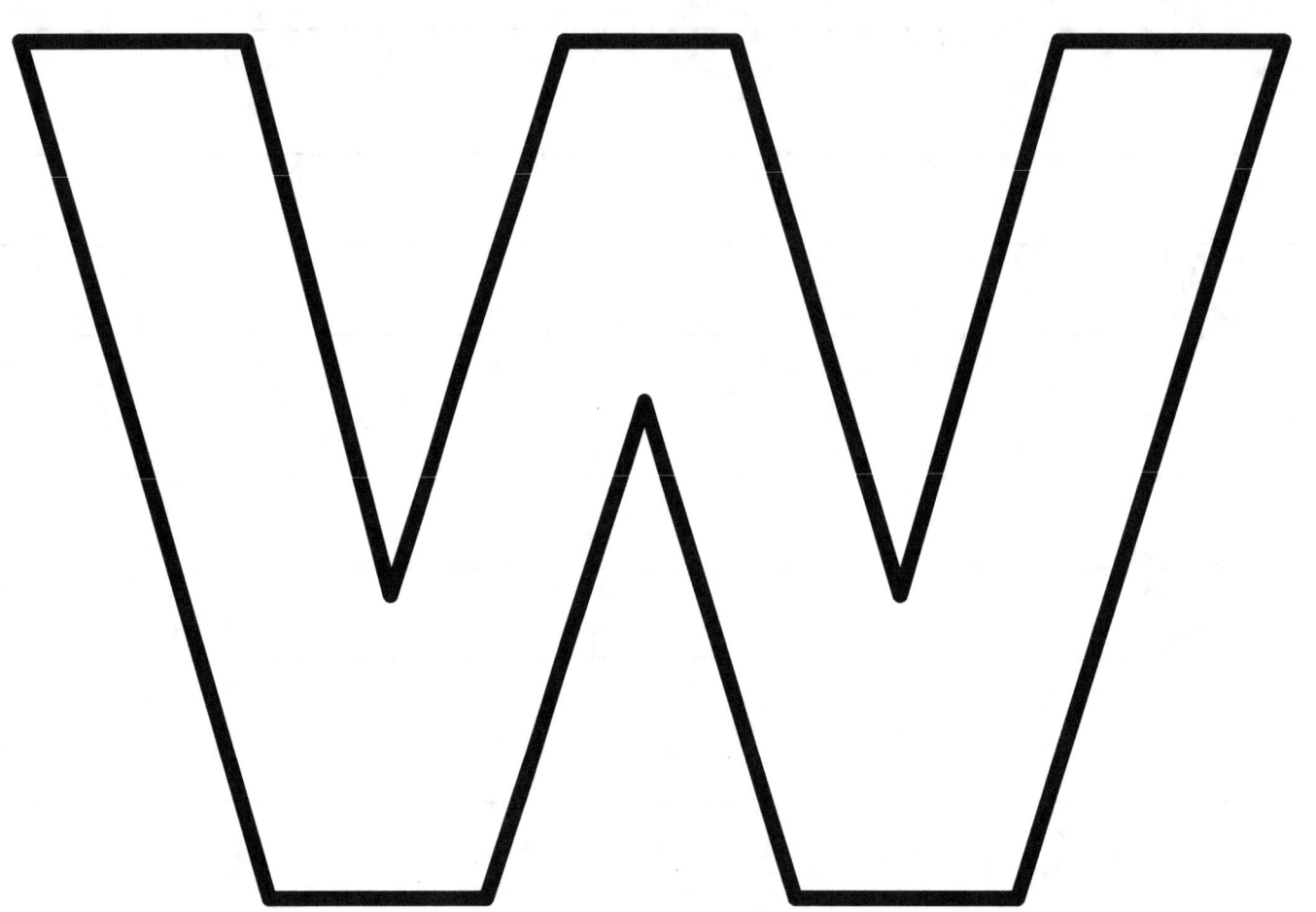

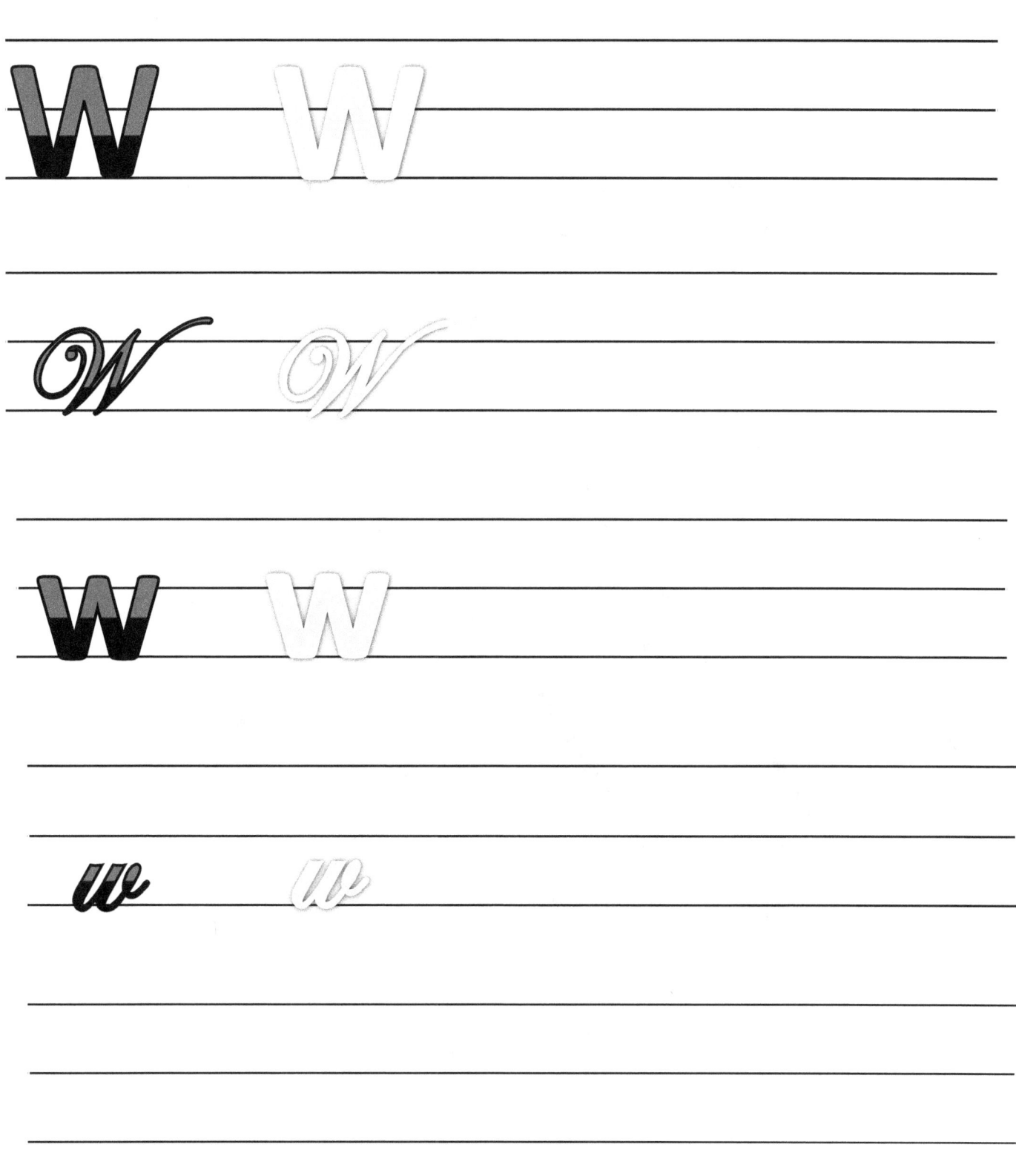

SAY & COLOR

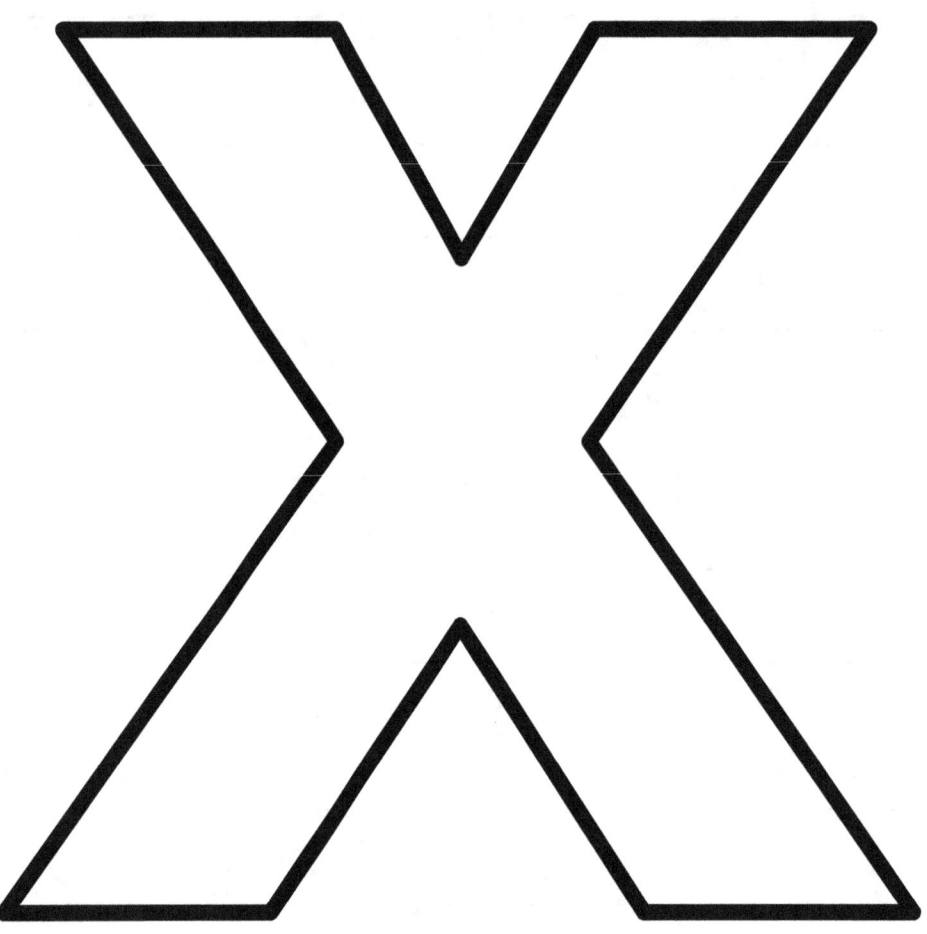

SAY & COLOR

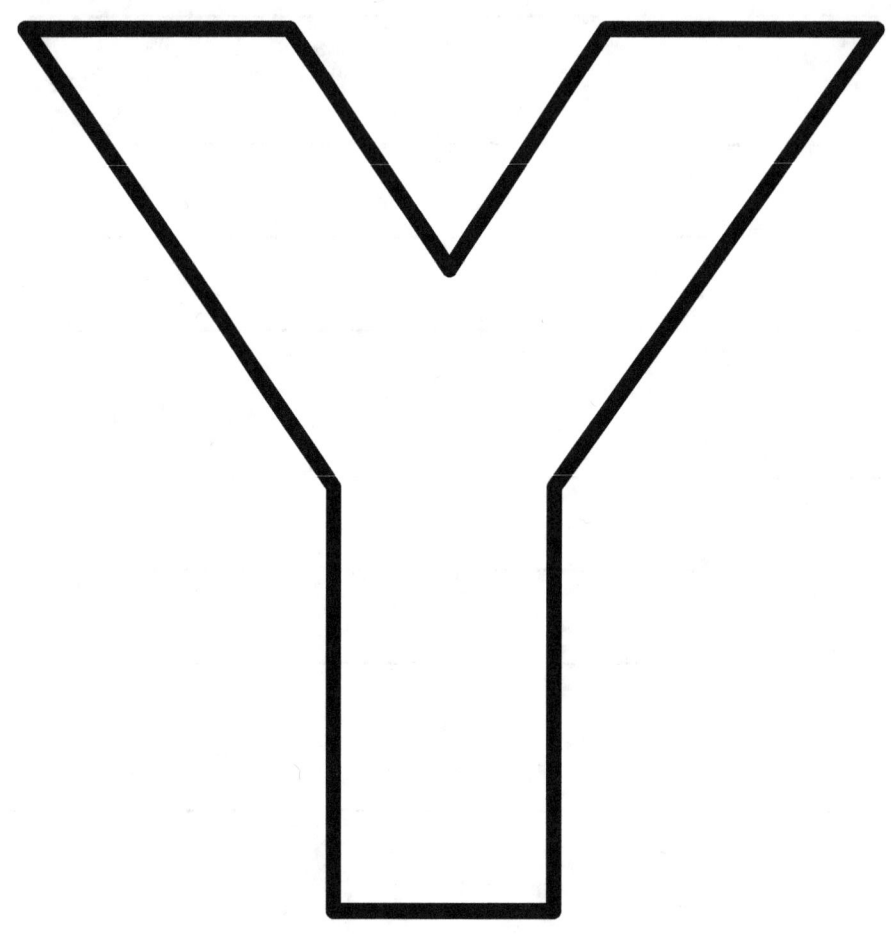

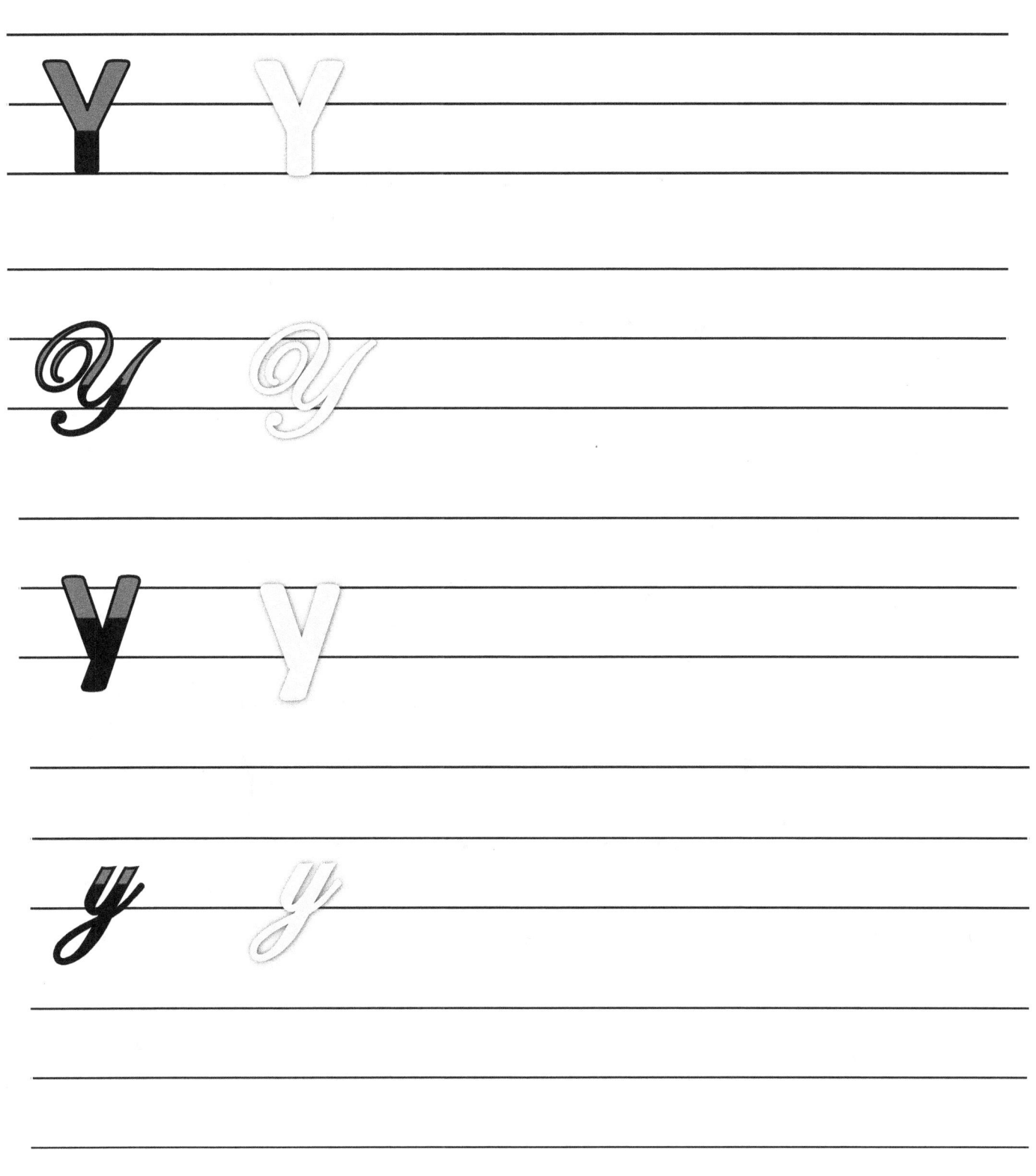

SAY & COLOR

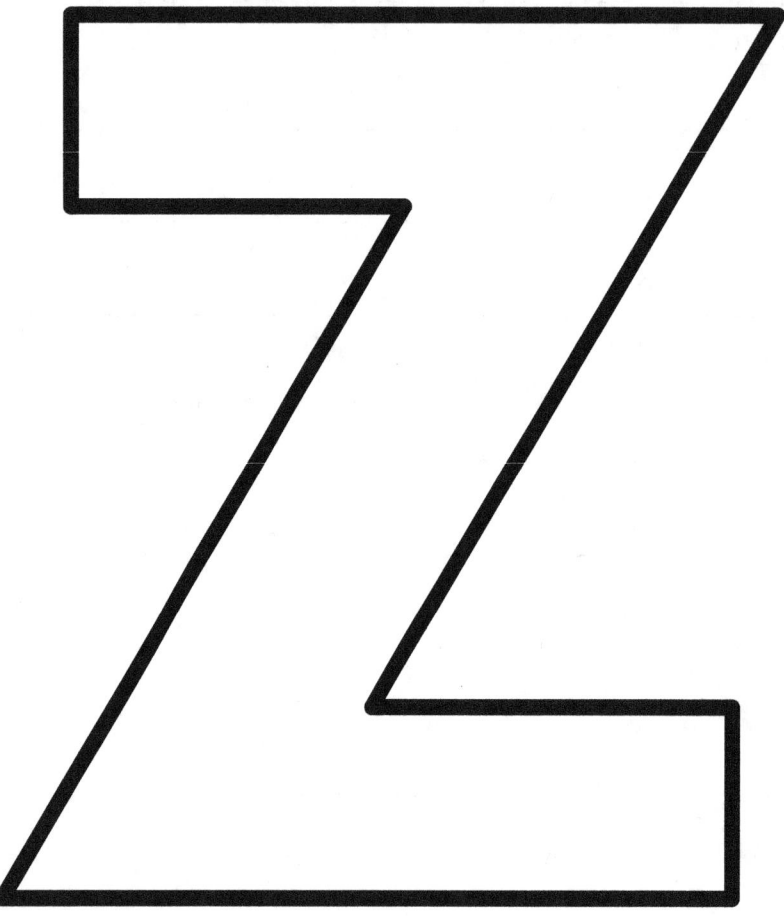

Z Z

Z Z

Z Z

Z Z

PRACTICING

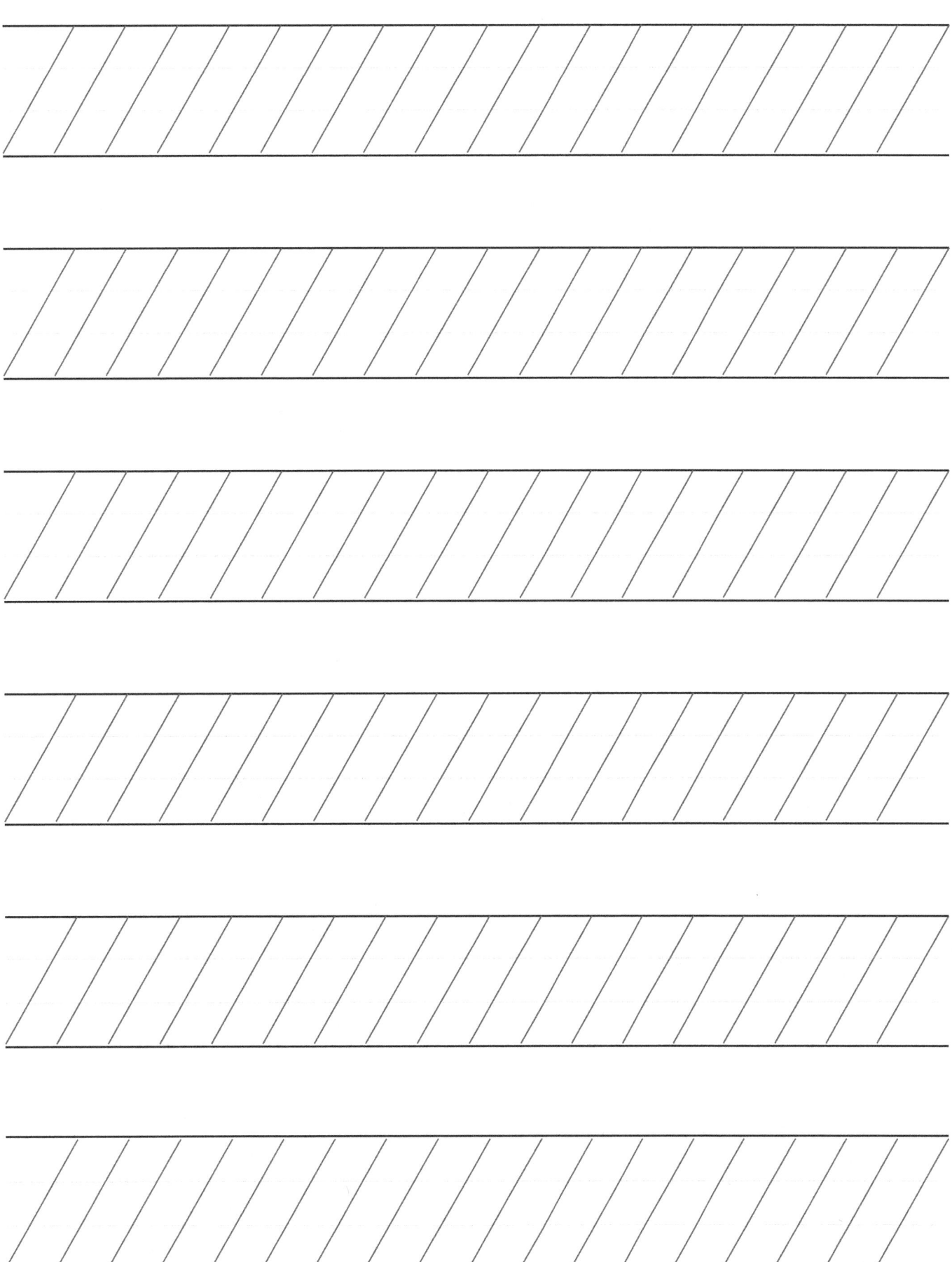

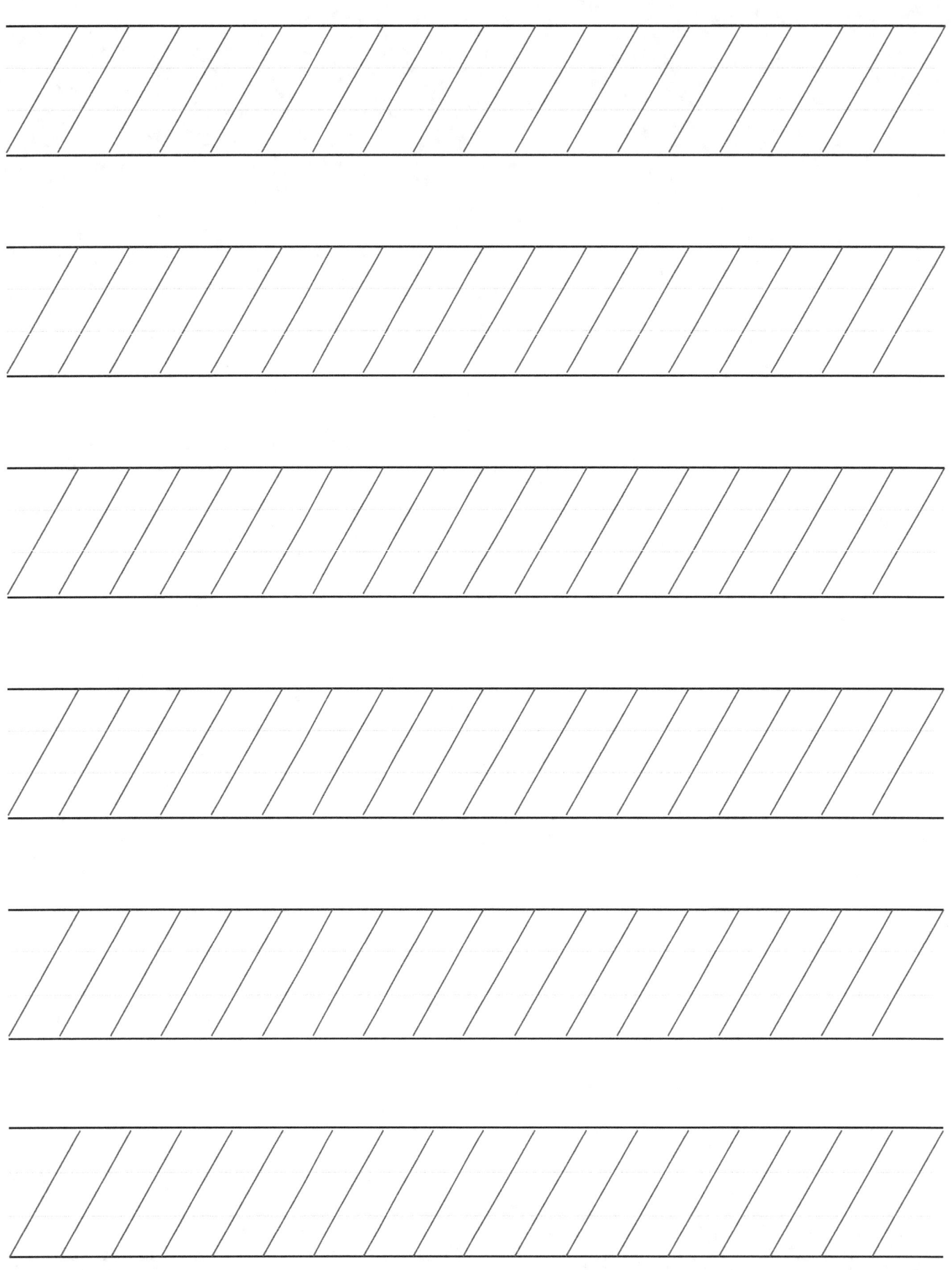

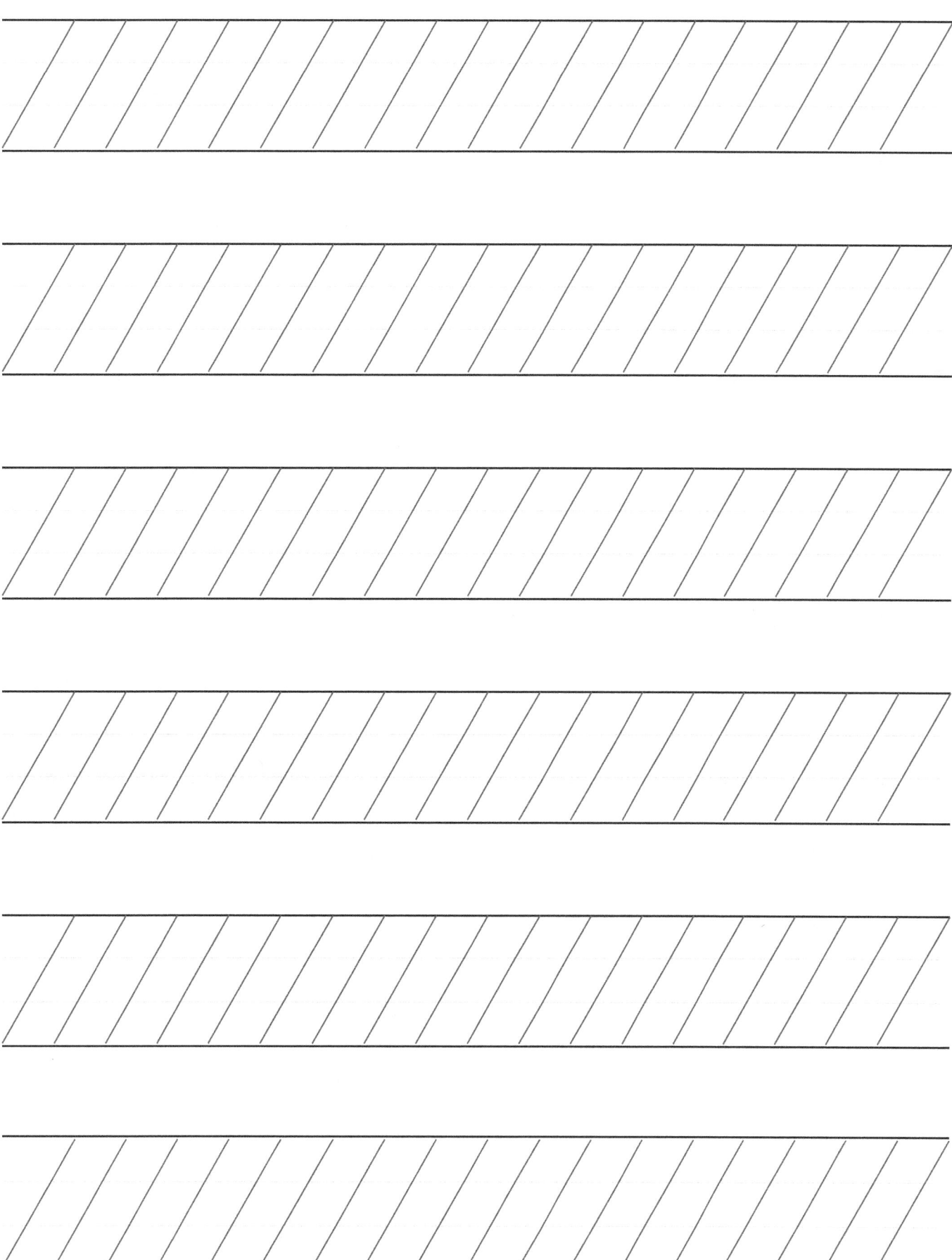

ANAS.sb publishing